EARNED

EARNED

THE TRUE COST OF GREATNESS FROM ONE
OF HOCKEY'S FIERCEST COMPETITORS

CHRIS PRONGER

MDP
MISSION
DRIVEN PRESS

DEDICATION

To Lauren, Jack, George, and Lilah—my greatest team.

You are the reason behind everything I do, the constant source of love, strength, and inspiration that has carried me through every chapter of my life. From the brightest moments of triumph to the hardest battles I've faced, you have been there—steady, supportive, and unwavering.

Lauren, your love and belief in me have been my anchor. You've walked beside me through every high and low, and your strength and grace have lifted me more times than I can count. To Jack, George, and Lilah—you've given me purpose far greater than the game. Watching you grow, chase your own dreams, and become the incredible people you are today has been my proudest accomplishment.

You are my foundation, the ones who keep me grounded when life gets overwhelming and remind me what truly matters. Without your love, encouragement, and patience, none of this—on the ice or beyond it—would have been possible.

This book, like every achievement in my life, belongs to you as much as it does to me. My gratitude and love for each of you will forever live in my heart.

To my mom and dad, Jim and Eila—thank you for everything.

From my earliest days on the ice, you were there, giving your time, your energy, and your love so that I could chase a dream. You sacrificed so much during my formative years—traveling countless miles, sitting through long practices and games, supporting me through every high and low. None of it ever seemed too much for you, and I know now just how much you gave up so I could have the chance to succeed.

Your love and guidance have been the steady hand at my back through every stage of life. When I stumbled, you picked me up. When I was riding high, you reminded me to stay humble and keep striving for more. Through it all, you believed in me, even when I didn't always believe in myself.

This journey, and this book, would not be possible without you. Everything I've achieved, I owe to you. I love you very much—thank you.

To my brother Sean—

From the very beginning, you were the one I looked up to, the one I wanted to be like. We battled as brothers do—fierce competitors in everything we touched—but those battles lit a fire in me that would never burn out. You were the spark behind my competitive edge, the drive that became my will to win.

Looking back, I know those moments were about more than just competing. They were about you pulling the best out of me, even when I didn't realize it. You pushed me, challenged me, and in doing so, showed me what it meant to dig deeper, to fight harder, and to never settle.

Thank you for paving the way, for letting me watch your journey, and for giving me the belief that I could carve out one of my own. Those lessons shaped me more than you'll ever know.

I'm grateful for every battle, every lesson, and every memory we share. Love you, bro.

CONTENTS

FOREWORD

By Teemu Selänne

played professional hockey for twenty two years. One memory that sticks out loud and clear is when I heard Chris Pronger (who I now call Prongs) and I would be on the same team. I found out on my birthday. It was July 3, 2006. I will never forget it.

I was in Finland, and the PR guy for the Anaheim Ducks called and said, "We've got Pronger."

I thought he meant *Sean* Pronger. I had been friends with Sean and played with him for a lot of years, so I was excited. When I figured out he meant Chris, I was shocked because I didn't even think he was available.

And then I was a little nervous.

That family is such a great family, so nice, I thought. *But it's got one asshole, and that's Chris.*

Prongs and I had battled back and forth for ten years on the ice—screaming at each other across hallways outside of locker rooms, on the Olympic team, on the ice. Hurting each other with our sticks and with our words. I normally didn't get personal with players, but when we went at each other, it did feel personal. We had a history of being at war.

Even with all that, when I heard he was joining the team, I thought: *Now we have the missing piece that we need. We have a chance to win the Cup.*

That's hockey for you.

See, when you played against Chris, you knew it was going to be hard. You knew you would have bruises, but that's why he was so good. He was always competing with everything he had. He would never show up halfway.

Our first practice together as teammates, after all the nasty stuff we used to yell at each other, Prongs walked over to me and opened up his arms.

"Teemu, give me a hug!"

After that, we became not just teammates but great friends. I was relieved when I figured out that it was never personal, just business. One thing that stands out from that time is how much of a pro Prongs was. He set an example for how to be a leader. Every time he opened his mouth, you knew you'd better listen. And he showed up prepared. He did what it took to play at that level—staying healthy, doing the right things on and off the ice, and staying committed. He set the standards very high and found a way to show up every day. Sometimes he got out of composure and took some penalties, yeah. But that was part of his personality and part of the game. Sometimes people need to wake up when they're not playing well. So he woke them up.

I also learned that off the ice, Prongs cared. He was always a true teammate, and he would do whatever it took to protect me and the rest of the guys. You could tell he truly enjoyed coming to the rink every day. We all had a mission, and we tried to remind each other every day that we might not ever get a chance like that again. There's never "next game, next year, next season"— we had to leave it all out there *in the present,* and then whatever happened, happened. You can always live with yourself if you've given it all you've got.

We *did* give it everything, and the next year—in 2007—we won the Stanley Cup. Prongs held it over his head after we beat the Ottawa Senators, and he handed it to me next. I'll never forget it. I remember thinking about a sign I'd seen in the crowd when the New York Rangers won it in '94. An older guy held it up, and it said: "Now, I can die in peace."

I had that same feeling. One of the best moments of my life, a dream come true. And it felt amazing to do it with those guys. When you battle together and win together like that, you become like family.

Hockey is the greatest sport because even guys who fight, even the enforcers, have so much respect for each other. They know it's just a game. When I came into the league as a young guy, I came from Europe where the culture of the game is a little different. I was shocked that these guys would fight and then go to the bar after to have drinks together. Then I realized that everybody knew it was just a job, just part of it.

Prongs and I are still close friends. I've known him for decades at this point. Over the years, I've watched him create his own family. He does everything for them, and it's beautiful to see.

And one thing I appreciate is that he's one of those guys who finds a way to win, whether it's in business or in life. I've seen him sacrifice and set standards for himself and his teammates. I've seen him use adversity to his advantage. I've seen him prepare like a madman and commit to getting better every day. No excuses.

We all want to win. In hockey, there are seven hundred other players who want to win too. It's not an easy thing. But winners find a way.

Prongs is a great role model for finding a way to win, and the same things that got him there apply across sports, business, and relationships. That's why I think this book is great because it means other people can learn these lessons that I've seen Prongs actually live every single game, every single year.

Why wouldn't you listen to a guy like that? We could all learn something.

INTRODUCTION

Hartford, Connecticut. 1995. The boos cascade down from every corner of the arena like an avalanche of disappointment. They're not booing the other team. They're booing me.

Fifteen thousand fans in the Civic Center, and in that moment, it felt like all of them hated me.

I'm twenty years old, making millions as the Hartford Whalers' supposed "franchise player in the making," and I'm getting destroyed by my own fans. In my own building. The noise is so loud it feels physical, like getting checked into the boards over and over again.

"Not worth the money!" someone screams from behind the bench.

He's not wrong.

I'd been drafted second overall in 1993. The city and owner expected a savior. What they got was an erratic, inconsistent player who couldn't figure out why his talent wasn't enough. I was supposed to be the cornerstone. Instead, I was crumbling.

That season in Hartford was when I first understood a truth that would take me years to fully grasp: Talent only gets you to the door. Staying there, succeeding there, leading there—that comes down to something else. Over the course of my career, I learned that success doesn't hinge on raw skill. It hinges on three things:

- Standards: the daily choices you set for yourself, the expectations you refuse to compromise.
- Adversity: the ability to turn setbacks into stepping stones.
- Ownership: the moment you stop blaming others and take full responsibility for your path.

Early on, I was just a tall, raw defenseman trying to figure things out. My real turning point came when a sports psychologist asked me a simple question: "What are your standards?" I didn't have an answer, but that question—and the process of finding the answer—changed everything.

I began to understand how those three principles worked together. Standards without adversity leave you untested. Adversity without ownership leaves you bitter. Ownership without standards leaves you directionless. But when you combine them—Standards + Adversity +

Ownership—that's where growth happens. That's where success is built.

This isn't a book of theories. It's the lessons I earned the hard way: while winning, while losing, while injured, and while in my best shape. Along the way I bet on myself and backed it up with work—and discovered that the road less traveled can still take you exactly where you need to go.

I'm not here to give you my exact roadmap—your standards, your adversity, your ownership will look different from mine. But I am here to show you how I learned to define them for myself, and how you can too.

Because talent might open the door, but it's these three principles that keep it open. And the good news is, they're available to anyone willing to commit.

But to figure out where we're going, it's helpful to look at where we've been. And hell, I've sure been around.

Over my nineteen-year NHL career, I played 1,167 regular season games and another 173 playoff games in the NHL. Won a Stanley Cup with Anaheim in 2007. Was inducted into the Hockey Hall of Fame in 2015. I could throw a lot more stats at you, but those aren't the numbers that matter. The number that matters most is *four*—those four words the sports psychologist asked me in 1995 that changed everything: "What are your standards?"

I couldn't answer him. After three years in the NHL, after being traded to St. Louis for their fan favorite Brendan Shanahan, after all the scouts had said I had talent, I couldn't name a single standard I held myself to. No wonder I was drowning under the pressure.

Here's what nobody tells you about success: It's not about working hard. Everyone works hard at this level. It's not about wanting it more, either. Everyone wants it. Success comes down to the standards you set when no one's watching and your ability to maintain them when everyone is.

Success comes down to the standards you set when no one's watching and your ability to maintain them when everyone is.

The road to success runs straight through the gates of adversity and requires ownership. There's no bypass. No shortcut. No easy route. You either embrace the difficulty, or you end up listening to thousands of people telling you exactly how much "you suck!" while caving under the weight of expectations.

In those early years, I made every mistake you can make. Relied on talent instead of discipline. Chose comfort over growth. Blamed everyone except the guy in the mirror. Let success go to my head and failure eat me alive. Used the victimhood mentality as a way to keep my sanity. Nearly destroyed my career before it really began.

In 1998, I almost died on the ice. Took a slap shot directly to the heart during a playoff game against Detroit. *Commotio cordis*—my heart stopped. The trainer couldn't find a pulse. My lips were starting to turn blue. By the grace of God, I came back to life. I took a deep gasp of air, and my heart restarted. I played again forty-eight hours later because that's what you do when you love something more than you fear dying for it.

But here's the thing about close calls—they're just wake-up calls you can't ignore. The question is whether you'll answer.

This book is about the decisions that saved my career and, more importantly, my life. It's about learning that champions behave like champions before they become champions. It's about understanding that standards, adversity, and ownership determine the success you get. Period.

If you picked up this book, you're probably in one of three places.

Maybe you're successful but stuck, knowing there's another level but not sure how to reach it.

Maybe you're struggling, wondering why your talent isn't translating to results.

Or maybe you've hit your own version of rock bottom and you're looking for a way back up.

Wherever you are, I've been there. And I can tell you this: The same principles that took me from being booed in Hartford to raising the Stanley Cup and winning the Hart Trophy apply whether you're on the ice, in the boardroom, or just trying to build a better life.

But I need to warn you about something. This book will challenge you. It's supposed to. Growth doesn't come from comfort. If you're looking for feel-good bullshit about believing in yourself, put this down now. If you want someone to tell you it's not your fault, I'm not your guy.

What I *will* give you is the truth about what it takes to transform potential into performance. The mindset that wins. The standards that separate those who talk about success from those who achieve it.

You'll learn why discipline beats motivation every time. How to turn adversity into your greatest advantage. Why owning your failures is the first step to real success. How to build standards that become your foundation when everything else shakes.

Discipline beats motivation every time.

Most importantly, you'll learn that you already have everything you need. You just haven't set the standards to access it yet.

One of the most defining lessons I learned came later in life: In the business of professional sports, you're only as good as your last game. You might as well be a piece of meat, so do a damn good job and then go on home. Remember where your priorities lie—which is a lesson for us all, not just my fellow athletes. (For me, it's family first, all the way.)

Another life-changing decision I made came in Dallas in October 2023—the choice to quit drinking alcohol. It wasn't just a lifestyle change. It was a complete reframe of how I saw myself, how I operated, and what I valued. In hindsight, the clarity that came after was staggering. Patterns emerged. Pain I had buried became visible. And while it wasn't always pretty, it was necessary. That journey, and the reflection it sparked, is a central part of this book. You don't have to take that same journey, but I'm sharing mine because I know it will open up your eyes to what you might not realize is right in front of you.

When it comes to realigning your life to your standards, I can't promise you it'll be easy. But I can promise it will be worth it . . . and that you can win in the end. And look, say what you want about me, but you sure as hell can't say I don't know how to win.

Ultimately the boos that almost broke me became the foundation for everything I achieved. Your biggest challenges right now? They're not obstacles. They're opportunities. But only if you're willing to do what most won't: take complete ownership of where you are and commit to the standards that will get you where you want to go.

So let me ask you the same question that changed my life: What are your standards?

And what is your relationship with ownership and adversity?

If you can't answer that right now, don't worry. By the time you finish this book, you will be able to.

The puck has dropped. The transformation starts now.

ACT I

Foundation and Fall

CHAPTER 1

Betting on Myself

The bus smells like wet hockey gear and teenage ambition. We're heading back from Fort Frances, a two-hour ride through Northwestern Ontario, and the energy is electric. We just beat them in their own barn, and now the euchre game in the back is getting loud. Someone's trying to harmonize with the boom box. It's my sophomore year playing for the Dryden Eagles, and this beat-up yellow bus carrying our high school team is exactly where I want to be.

My buddy had slid into the seat next to me, gear bag hitting the floor with a thud. We've played together since we were kids, and he knows me well enough to get straight to the point.

"You still think you made the right call? Everyone else your age is playing AAA."

I look out the window at the frozen Canadian Shield landscape blurring past. It's a question I've been asked a hundred times since I chose high school hockey over AAA. Every scout, every coach, every hockey parent in Dryden has an opinion about my decision.

"If I'm good enough, they'll find me."

He shakes his head. "That's not how it works, and you know it."

Maybe he's right. The traditional path to the NHL is clear: play AAA, get noticed by junior scouts, get drafted to the Ontario Hockey League (OHL), then hope you're good enough for the show. By staying in high school, I'm playing fewer games—maybe thirty compared to sixty in AAA. Limited ice time. Fewer scouts in the stands.

But here's what everyone criticizing my decision doesn't understand: I'm not following anyone else's path. I'm betting on myself and betting on my ability to play at a high level while also having the ability to play with my friends and be a teenager.

Let me take you back to where this started.

I grew up watching my brother, Sean, play. He was two years older, and like most younger brothers, I wanted to do everything he did. My brother and I would play hockey every single day, whether it was road hockey in front of our house, in the driveway shooting pucks, or down in our basement throwing a ball in the corner and seeing who could come up with it. (More often than not, it was Sean.) Hockey was something that we both loved to do, and we were able to push one another.

I am almost certain that having an older brother helped prepare me to always want to level up and compete and challenge myself—because I needed that push. I was challenged every day playing against older kids and playing against my brother, who was really good . . . and I hated to lose. I was a tall kid, super skinny, and I needed to figure out how to hang with the big boys. As I look back, I can't help but smile, even though there were certainly the occasional fits of crying when we were little and more than a handful of bloody noses, probably making the people driving by cringe. Even through the blood and tears, we were usually still laughing, having the time of our lives. Out of all the things I've done in my career, those times are some of my favorite memories of playing hockey—ever.

When we got older, Sean went the traditional route—the "right" path—play AAA in Kenora, then Junior A with the Thunder Bay Flyers before getting a scholarship to play NCAA hockey at BGSU. I watched him leave for those ten- to twelve-hour bus rides to Thompson and all those other northern towns in Manitoba. I saw the toll it took. The grind. Long weekends. Family time sacrificed.

When it came time for me to make the same decision, everyone expected me to follow in Sean's footsteps. I was fourteen. Playing AAA meant three hours round-trip to Kenora for every practice, every home game . . .

and then even longer rides for road games. It meant my parents' lives revolving around my hockey schedule. It meant leaving behind the team and friends that I'd grown up with. I wanted some sort of a normal high school experience, which was the opposite of what I'd seen with Sean.

"You'll never make it playing high school hockey," the Kenora coach told me when I declined their offer. "You're wasting your talent up there. This is a mistake. You're going to regret it."

I was asked multiple times to reconsider. People pointed at my brother, who was now playing junior hockey in Thunder Bay, and other kids from Dryden who'd gone the AAA route. But I wasn't worried about what they were telling me. It was more about the experience I was looking for and carving my own path. I wasn't thinking about junior hockey yet. I was thinking about playing with my friends who were older (my brother's age) so the competition level would be greater.

But I also saw something others didn't. Our high school team had eight or nine guys who could really play. We had older kids coming back from junior opportunities—nineteen- and twenty-year-olds who'd been cut from junior teams and who outweighed me both in size and ability at the time. I used the older kids as a gauge to see where I was, relative to them, constantly trying to improve.

Besides that, we had Jack McMaster.

Jack was my defense coach—my D coach—and he'd played both university and senior-league hockey. He was the first real coach I'd had who really knew what it took to play at a high level, and he became one of my most important early mentors. My dad had also played old-timers hockey with our head coach, who also happened to be vice principal of the high school. That familiarity with the coaching staff certainly played a part in my parents' supporting my decision.

Jack, in particular, saw something in me—the raw talent, plus the willingness to put in the work and be coached. The fire in my eyes and the desire to want to learn, to be a sponge. When a great coach sees that, I believe they get excited about helping you become successful . . . at least, that's the way it was with Jack. Jack worked with me in grades nine and ten, from 1988 to 1990, which were very formative years in my hockey career. Even then, I knew how special it was to have him in my corner, and he's still somebody I love connecting with and talking hockey with to this day. We have a great deal of mutual respect for each other.

I can still remember the first practice of that high school season: I went out there unsure of myself and not committing to my game. I was already six one and growing. These were mostly the same kids I'd been playing with forever. I knew their moves, their weaknesses. This would be a cakewalk.

I was wrong.

Jack pulled me aside after that first practice. "You've got raw talent," he said. "But you're relying on your size. You telegraph your passes. Your positioning needs work."

Every day after practice, Jack would stay on the ice with me. He'd sit with me on bus rides, in the locker room, after games. We'd talk about the game, about life, about his experience playing at the university level and in senior hockey. The fact that he really took the time to work with me on my game on and off the ice was pivotal in knowing I made the right decision. He also looked out for me, knowing we had a number of older guys on the team.

"When a coach invests time in you because they see something," he told me, "soak up everything."

And I did.

After my freshman year, I went to try out for the Thunder Bay Flyers, where my brother was playing. I got cut because they thought I was too young and not ready for the long grind of their season. I was slight and needed to add some weight, sure, but I'd thought I could get past that issue. In my training camp exit meeting, they told me they would love to have me come play for them the next year. That sealed the deal for me—I was going back to high school to play.

Playing against those older guys—giving up fifty pounds to some of them—forced me to use my leverage and guile over brute strength. When you can't just muscle your way through, you have to see the ice differently. Anticipate instead of react. Play chess while they're playing checkers.

My sophomore year was special. We did an exchange program with a school from St. John's, Newfoundland. Spent a week there, lived with a family, and played against their team. Those bus rides with our new friends were filled with laughter, card games, and the kind of camaraderie you can't manufacture. During a playoff game against Fort Frances, something just took me over. Before the start of overtime, as we came back onto the ice, I skated toward our fans—they'd driven over two hours to support us—and slammed myself against the glass to fire them up. We won in overtime and advanced. What a rush that was!

I think back to how simple life was back in high school. Not long after, hockey would become a job with pressure and stress. But in those moments, on those bus rides to Kenora or Fort Frances, preparing to play with my friends and teammates, it was pure joy. Hockey was always a love for me, a way to get my energy out—whether it was my brother, Sean, and I playing road hockey with our friends at our house, playing at the outdoor rink down the street, or knocking each other around in our basement when it was too dark or cold to go out. I studied the game with a passion, in awe of the guys who came before me. As a kid, I could recite every draft pick from years back. Later, when I grew up and had an agent, he would look at me and say, "How the hell did you know that?" when I rattled off some obscure draft fact. My whole life, when things got complicated, one fact was always certain for me: On the ice, I knew what was happening. On the ice, I could put my focus and my extra energy into something and dominate.

For a small-town high school team like Dryden, just making it to OFSAA, the provincial championships in Ontario, was remarkable—and we made it both my freshman and sophomore years. It helped that I grew up practicing against top players in the game: Sean, who went on to play at Bowling Green State University and then in the NHL for eleven years; my D partner, Chris Hancock, who played Junior B in Barrie and then college hockey at Union; and Darcy Mitani, who went on to play at the University of North Dakota and had a fifteen-year professional career in Japan. You don't see that often from a small town like ours out in the middle of nowhere—that many players advancing to higher levels. It's something our hometown of Dryden takes great pride in. That's where everything changed.

My sophomore year at OFSAA, we lost a heartbreaker in the semifinals to end our championship hopes, but I'd played at another level throughout the tournament. At that point, I had become our best player. I'd grown to around six three and was a strong skater, mobile, agile, and physical. I didn't do a lot of work in the weight room (yet), but I worked my ass off in practice to allow for growth in my game. I was very confident in my decision-making as my understanding of the game continued to grow.

In late spring 1990, I set my sights on Team Ontario and the Canada Winter Games. I went to the regional tryout camp but was cut because I hadn't prepared physically. Luckily for me, though, the right person had been in the stands during that OFSAA tournament: Sheldon Ferguson, a Team Ontario scout and head of Central Scouting at the time. He took a chance on the tall, lanky defenseman from Dryden and used a wild card spot to get me into the main camp in Toronto.

"You've got that chip on your shoulder," he told me. "Keep it. You'll need it."

That chip grew. I trained hard and showed up ready for *this* Team Ontario tryout camp and ended with a great showing. I made the team and pulled on that jersey for the Canada Winter Games—the first time I'd played on a national stage. That February and early March of 1991, we went up against the best seventeen-and-under players from every province.

The following summer, I took another leap—this time wearing the maple leaf for Canada's Under-18 team at a tournament in Japan. It was my first taste of international hockey, lining up against the best players my age in the world—a life-changing experience. Making this All-Star team in my first foray and proudly wearing the maple leaf on my chest is something I'll never forget.

I actually felt comfortable at that level—against players in my age group who were going into their draft years highly rated in the first round.

When I got home, the next decision was waiting: Should I stay on the college track and play NCAA hockey in the US, or take a shot at major junior hockey in Canada? The Peterborough Petes, of the Ontario Hockey League (OHL), had drafted me that spring, and in August I had my forty-eight-hour tryout window—just long enough to skate with them without losing NCAA eligibility. I decided to go to see if it was the right fit.

From the moment I stepped on the ice in Peterborough, I knew it was. The pace, the competition, the atmosphere—it felt like the next level I'd been chasing. Later, Jeff Twohey—the assistant coach—remembered how Dick Todd, the head coach, had responded to watching me play:

"I still clearly remember Dick skating over to me during your first practice and saying to me, 'Have you seen what Pronger's doing on the ice? We have a nineteen-year-old defenseman that can't do what he can do.' My reply? 'No shit, Sherlock!'"

I had a great relationship with Jeff "Dew" Twohey. Later on in Peterborough, he and I were generally the first ones on the ice and the last ones off. I'd sit with him on long bus rides, talking through scouting reports and lineups. I loved learning from him, working on little things. (I was such a student of the game that once I even corrected Dick Todd on the lineup for an opposing team during warm-ups . . . something I'm not sure I'd recommend, but I did it anyway.)

Looking back, that decision to bet on myself set a pattern for every major decision in my life. What was I learning? Trust your gut, but back it up with action. Mentors matter. Preparation matters. And sometimes, when you take the road less traveled, it leads you exactly where you need to go.

Trust your gut, but back it up with action.

A couple years later, when I had to choose between the NCAA and the OHL, I'd remember this lesson. When I was struggling in Hartford, getting booed by my own fans, I'd remember that the path to success isn't always the one everyone else is taking. When I had to rebuild my career from scratch, I'd remember that betting on yourself isn't about taking the easy way—it's about taking your way and then working twice as hard to prove it was the right one.

I think sometimes we fall into the trap of thinking we need to follow the exact path others took. *My brother did it this way, so I should too.* But you have to know yourself—your unique characteristics, your mindset, your personality. How does that fit with what's being presented to you?

My dad understood this. He could have easily steered me toward AAA like Sean. But he knew his kids. He had the backbone to not worry about what everybody else was doing and focus on what was best for me.

The standards you set determine the success you get. My first standard, before I even knew what standards were, was simple: I'll do it my way, and I'll outwork everyone to prove my way works.

Twenty-five years later, with a Stanley Cup ring, two Olympic gold medals, and a Hockey Hall of Fame jacket in my closet, I can tell you it was a bet worth making.

But first, I had to prove those coaches wrong.

CHAPTER 2

Fork in the Road

The puck hit the post with a crack that echoed through the empty arena. It was August 1991 in Peterborough, and I was sharing the ice with guys who'd been playing in the show while I was still doing homework. Three current NHLers. Five drafted players. And me—a seventeen-year-old kid who wasn't even supposed to be here.

The Petes' head coach, Dick Todd, had worn me down. He'd been calling at least once a week since they'd drafted me in the sixth round—a pick everyone said they'd wasted on a kid bound for college. But here I was, betting on myself again, using my forty-eight-hour tryout window to see what I was missing.

I lined up for the next drill and found myself matched against a twenty-four-year-old forward who'd logged sixty games with the Toronto Maple Leafs the previous season. The guy had forty pounds on me, easy. The whistle blew. He came at me with that lazy confidence NHLers have in summer skates—like they're operating at 60 percent, and that's still more than enough.

Trust your gut, I told myself. *You earned your way here.*

I stepped up at the blue line, kept my feet moving, and threw a hip check that sent him spinning into the boards. Clean hit. Textbook even. The sound of his surprise—that little grunt when you don't see it coming—was worth whatever was coming next.

He got up slowly, shaking his head. "Little prick," he muttered, but there was something else in his eyes. Respect, maybe. Or at least acknowledgment that I wasn't just there to fill out numbers.

That's when it clicked. These guys weren't gods. They were human. Better than me, sure. More experienced, absolutely. But the gap? It wasn't the Grand Canyon I'd built up in my head. It was jumpable.

"Nice hit, rook," one of the drafted guys said, skating by.

Three more rushes, two more hits, and one assist later, I was keeping pace. Not dominating—let's not get carried away—but holding my own. By the end of the session, my legs were jelly and my lungs were burning, but something had shifted.

In the dressing room, I sat there unlacing my skates, replaying every drill and every shift. These were the guys

I'd watched on TV, collected their hockey cards. And I'd just gone toe to toe with them.

"Hey kid," the Leafs forward called over. "Where'd you play last year?"

"Junior B, the Stratford Cullitons," I said.

He laughed. "Junior B? Shit. Keep hitting like that, you won't be there long."

The drive back to my hotel took twenty minutes. Twenty minutes of my mind racing, replaying Dick Todd's words from our last phone call: "You're different, Chris. You bet on yourself playing high school instead of AAA. Now you're letting other people tell you what your next move should be."

They're not that much better than me.

The thought wouldn't leave. It burrowed in deep, challenging everything I thought I knew about the path I was supposed to take. The lesson? If you're good enough, they'll find you. Doesn't matter if you're playing in the middle of nowhere. Doesn't matter if you didn't follow their prescribed development path. Talent finds a way—but only if you're willing to bet on yourself first.

Talent finds a way—but only if you're willing to bet on yourself first.

THE MAN WHO WOULDN'T TAKE
NO FOR AN ANSWER

Dick Todd hadn't just called me after the draft. He'd launched a full campaign.

First week: "Just wanted to say congratulations on being drafted, Chris. Know you're planning on college, but the door's always open here."

Second week: "Heard you've been skating in Dryden. Staying sharp. That's good. That's the kind of commitment we value in Peterborough."

By the third week, my mom knew his voice when she picked up the phone. (No caller ID back then.) "It's Dick again," she said to me. "Should I tell him you're out?"

"No, I'll take it."

Truth was, I liked talking to him. Unlike the college recruiters who sold me on their programs, Dick sold me on myself. Every conversation, he'd remind me of what I'd already proven—that the conventional path wasn't my path.

"You know what bugs me, Chris?" he said during one call. "You've spent your whole hockey life proving people wrong. Playing high school when they said play AAA. Making Team Ontario when they said you couldn't. Now you're about to do what everyone expects. That doesn't sound like the kid I've been watching."

"Maine is a great opportunity—"

And it was. Nobody knew it then, but there would be seven future NHL players on Maine's roster including Garth Snow, Mike Dunham, Patrice Tardif, Peter and Chris Ferraro, Jim Montgomery, and even my friend Paul Kariya who would have been a freshman with me. Outside of going to Bowling Green to play with my brother, Maine was looking pretty damn good.

"—for someone else," Dick cut in. "Not for you. You're not a four-year college player. You're a future NHL star who needs to play against the best competition every night. That's not Maine. That's the OHL."

I'd hang up after each call and stare at all the college-information packets on my desk. Everything laid out perfectly. Safe, smart, guaranteed education.

So why did it feel like I was settling?

"Just come visit," Dick said during what must have been our fourth call. "One day. Meet the organization, see the city, look at what we're building and see if you like it here. If you can look me in the eye after that and say you're not interested, I'll stop calling."

"Fine," I said. "One day."

"That's all I need."

A friend of Dick's picked me and my parents up in his small plane and flew us down to Peterborough. It was a tight squeeze, and I was nervous—we hit weather and had to stay over in Sault Ste. Marie. But we made it.

The Peterborough Memorial Centre sat right downtown, this old barn that had seen better days but wore its scars like badges of honor. Dick met us at the entrance, firm handshake, direct eye contact. No sales pitch. Just confidence.

"Before we go in," he said, "I want you to understand something. I don't chase players. In twenty years of coaching, I've never done what I've done with you. But sometimes you see something special, something different, and you've got to trust your gut. That's what I'm doing here."

Trust your gut. My words, coming back at me.

We walked through those doors, and I felt it immediately. This wasn't just a hockey rink. This was a proving ground. A place where boys became men, where potential became performance. The walls were covered with photos of Peterborough graduates. Yzerman. Gainey. Redmond.

And maybe, if I was willing to bet on myself one more time, Pronger.

And I was.

After seeing the town and talking to Dick, my parents, and my agent, I decided to give training camp a shot. I wanted to gauge where I was respective to the other top prospects. Back then, you had to pay your own way to go to training camp to keep your NCAA eligibility. For most players, it was a gamble; for me, it was an investment.

When I was skating with those guys, I realized something. *They're not that much better than me*, I thought. *I can at least hold my own here. And if I want to play with the best, I need to be challenged. If I go here, I get better. If I go back to Stratford, I might go backwards.*

And even back then, I knew there was only one way to go: up.

THE HOUSE THAT FELT LIKE HOME

At the end of the day, the Petes gave me a contract they had never given to anybody before—and have never since. My agent, Pat Morris, negotiated that they cover my schooling and a hell of a lot more. Because I was giving up a scholarship and a university opportunity, I needed to be covered on the education front on the back end . . . especially with the potential that I could get hurt.

Off the ice, I was a shy, tall kid. People stared all the time. The rink was my sanctuary, my safe place. After I signed the deal with the Petes, all I could make were brief public comments, mostly consisting of some muttering of my version of "thanks" and averting my eyes.

That great deal with the Petes meant I'd be living seventeen hundred kilometers away from home, still a kid. I needed to figure out the logistics, which meant I'd be living with a family, the Whites, Roger and Debbie. I would be their first Petes player.

That first night, Roger White answered the door and welcomed my parents and me inside. The house smelled like Sunday dinner at my grandmother's—roast beef, gravy, something sweet baking in the oven. Their sons—Chris and Greg—were setting the table, sneaking looks at the tall teenager who might be living in their spare room. Their two young daughters were playing, looking on.

"You must be Chris," Debbie said, wiping her hands on her apron before shaking mine. "Roger, get them drinks. Kids, say hello."

Here's what nobody tells you about leaving home (for the second time) at sixteen: The hockey part's easy. It's everything else that hits harder, something I'd learned when playing in Stratford twenty hours away from my hometown: Eating alone. Washing your own gear. Coming back to an empty room after a bad game with no one to talk to. That's what sends kids home with their tails between their legs.

Within five minutes at the Whites' dinner table, I knew this was different. Over dinner, I noticed my parents exchanging glances. This was the part they'd been dreading—handing their son over to strangers who were a long car ride away from home.

"What about when he's struggling?" Mom asked. "Hockey or . . . other things?"

"We handle it the same way you would," Debbie said. "With honesty. With boundaries. With support when they need it and a kick in the ass when they need that."

Roger's daughter climbed onto his lap halfway through dinner. He just kept eating one-handed, helping her cut her meat, natural as breathing. That's when I knew. This wasn't a business arrangement. This was a family that happened to have a spare room.

"Can I ask you something?" I said as Debbie brought out apple pie that made my mouth water.

"Shoot," Roger said.

"Why do you want to do this? Take in players?"

He considered it, really thought about his answer. "Because we wanted to support the team and thought this might be good for our boys."

After dinner, Debbie showed me the separate area above the garage. Nothing fancy but perfect for me—single bed, desk, closet, small TV with basic cable. But it was clean, had its own bathroom, and the window looked out on a backyard where I could already picture myself relaxing and getting some quiet time away from the rink.

"House rules," she said, businesslike now. "Curfew's 10 p.m. on school nights, midnight on weekends unless you have a game. No girls in the bedroom—living room's fine if we're home. No parties here, ever. Team parties happen somewhere else. We do your laundry twice a week, but this room stays clean or you do it yourself. Dinners at six when you're in town—you miss it, you make your own. Do you have any questions?"

"What if I screw up?"

She smiled. "Then you own it, we deal with it, and we move forward. But Chris? If you're ever in real trouble—any kind of trouble—you come to us first. Not your teammates, not your coach. Us. That's non-negotiable."

Walking back to the car, my parents were quiet. Finally, Mom spoke, tears welling up in her eyes. "They seem like good people."

"They are good people," Dad agreed.

What they weren't saying hung in the air: These strangers would do a better job preparing me for life than any college dorm supervisor. And after meeting them, my parents were at ease knowing the Whites would be looking out for me.

In the car, Dick Todd's earlier words echoed: "I'm not just offering you a place to play hockey. I'm offering you a place to become who you're supposed to be."

The Whites were proof he meant it.

This is an example of something crucial that would take me years to fully process: The fear of playing it safe is bigger than the fear of failing. The best decisions in life are rarely the sure ones. They're the ones that scare you just enough to know you're alive.

---

*The fear of playing it safe is bigger
than the fear of failing.*

THE PRICE OF CHOOSING

After I'd made my mind up, gone was the safe Chris Pronger who followed the expected path. What emerged was a different version—hungrier. Ready to prove that "the road less traveled" isn't just a pretty phrase in a poem. It's a competitive advantage if you're willing to pay the price. My license plate back then, the one with my nickname—Chaos—described me well. I was ready to fight when the time was right, full of energy and a desire to prove myself.

I started the phone calls at 9 a.m.

First, Maine. The assistant coach who'd recruited me couldn't hide his disappointment. "Chris, think about what you're giving up. The education. The experience. This is a decision you might regret."

"Maybe. But I'd regret not trying more."

Next, the other schools that had offered scholarships. Michigan. Denver. Bowling Green, where my brother played and where I was leaning. Each call the same dance—disappointment, attempts to change my mind, barely concealed frustration that a kid would choose the Petes over their program.

The local hockey community was rougher. Word travels fast in a small town. But the worst part? The doubt that crept in during quiet moments. Late at night, packing my life into bags, I'd wonder if they were right. If I was throwing away a sure thing for a dream. If I was just another delusional kid who thought he was better than he was.

That's when I'd remember that pre-camp summer skate in Peterborough—just before my official forty-eight-hour tryout window started. The NHLers. The gap that was jumpable. *Trust your gut, Chris. It's gotten you this far. There's no turning back now. Time to give it your all.*

Soon after, I was living at the Whites', practicing with the Petes, and playing against guys who'd been drafted by NHL teams. The pace was insane. The skill level, ridiculous. First practice, I was a step behind on everything. Second practice, half a step. By the first week, I was keeping up.

By the first month, I was excelling.

Dick Todd pulled me aside after a particularly good practice. "You know why I kept calling?"

"Because you're stubborn?"

"Because I saw something in you that you're just starting to see in yourself. You're not just a good player, Chris. You're different. You see the game differently. You approach it differently. College would have made you good. We're going to make you great."

That first season in Peterborough, I put up sixty-two points in sixty-three games. Led all rookie defensemen in scoring. NHL scouts were starting to notice, and the buzz for the draft was starting to percolate for next season. By Christmas, those same people who'd said I was making a mistake were asking for tickets to games.

Funny how that works.

But here's what that decision really taught me: Every transformative moment in your life will require you to disappoint someone. Usually multiple someones. The question is whether you're more willing to disappoint them or yourself.

Every transformative moment in your life will require you to disappoint someone.

I chose them. And that choice made all the difference.

THE COMPOUND EFFECT

Two years later, on June 26, 1993—draft day—I was sitting in a hotel room in Quebec City. Not watching it on TV like before—I was there, wearing my new draft suit, charcoal gray with a maroonish hue, waiting to hear my name called. (I got mixed reviews on my attire. Because I'm an admittedly tall and lanky guy, Don Cherry once said I looked like Ichabod Crane in a suit.)

That day, surrounded by my parents, grandparents, brother, and family friends, I had a lot of nervous energy. It wasn't about *if* I would go . . . it was *when* and *where*.

The hockey world's a funny place. Three years earlier, those evaluators said I wasn't good enough. The NCAA schools said I was making a mistake. And here I was, projected to go in the top three picks in the first round of the NHL draft.

"With the second overall pick, the Hartford Whalers select . . . Chris Pronger."

Second. Overall.

The walk to the stage felt like I was floating. Shaking hands with Brian Burke, the GM who'd just bet his franchise on a kid who'd taken the road less traveled. Pulling on that Whalers jersey. Cameras flashing. Mom crying. Dad stoic as ever. Hall of Famer Gordie Howe was even at the draft table. *Gordie Howe!* Wow, what a moment.

In the media scrum after, a reporter asked the question everyone was thinking: "Chris, you could've been playing college hockey right now. Any regrets about choosing the OHL?"

I looked him straight in the eye and replied with the sass that I would become known for in the media. "I'm standing here as the second overall pick. What do you think?"

But here's what I didn't say: It wasn't just about where I got drafted. It was about who I'd become in those two years in the OHL and one year in Junior B. The OHL didn't just make me a better hockey player. It made me comfortable being uncomfortable. It taught me that iron sharpens iron, but only if you're willing to get cut a few times.

Dick Todd found me after the interviews. "Keep trusting your gut. The hard choices don't stop here— they just get bigger."

He was right, of course. That Hartford jersey I'd just pulled on? I'd wear it for only two seasons before another fork in the road appeared. Then St. Louis. Then Edmonton. Then Anaheim. Then Philadelphia. Each trade, each decision, each moment of uncertainty, another opportunity to prove myself.

Even that first big milestone—getting drafted—was only the starting line. In the weeks that followed, I'd learn something every young player eventually figures out: *Being drafted doesn't mean you've made it.* It means you've been noticed. There were contracts to sign, camps to survive, expectations to meet—and pressure from every direction. I didn't know it yet, but that first summer would test me more than any game I'd ever played.

THE THREAD THAT RUNS THROUGH

Twenty-five years after that draft day, I can trace a direct line from every major success in my life back to the moment I chose discomfort over comfort. High school over AAA. OHL over NCAA. Fighting through injuries when quitting would've been easier. Taking ownership when blaming others was tempting.

The thread that runs through it all? Simple: When faced with a choice between what's expected and what's possible, choose possible. Even if—especially if—it scares the shit out of you.

---

*When faced with a choice between
what's expected and what's possible,
choose possible. Even if—especially
if—it scares the shit out of you.*

Because here's what I know now that I didn't know then: Every person who's achieved anything significant has a story. A moment when they stood at their own fork in the road and chose the path that demanded more of them.

Maybe yours isn't about hockey. Maybe it's about leaving a safe job to start a business. Walking away from a relationship that's comfortable but not right. Moving across the country for an opportunity. Going back to school. Having that difficult conversation. Making that investment in yourself.

The details don't matter. The decision does.

YOUR FORK IS WAITING

Let me ask you what Dick Todd asked me all those years ago: Are you doing what everyone expects, or are you doing what you're truly capable of?

If you're standing at your own fork in the road, here's my advice—what I learned from a lifetime of standards, adversity, and ownership:

- Set your **standard** before the moment tests you. Fear will show up—it always does. The goal isn't to erase it, but to have standards strong enough to steady you when it hits. Talent bends under pressure; standards hold.

- **Adversity** is the proof, not the punishment. When things get hard, that's life checking whether your standards are real or just words on paper. Every setback—boos, injuries, doubt—isn't a detour; it's the training ground for the next level.

- **Own** your choice and your response. No excuses. No "what-ifs." Every decision carries a cost, and you don't get to control the outcome—but you always control your effort and your attitude. Ownership isn't about being perfect; it's about being accountable when you're not.

That kid who chose high school hockey became a second-overall draft pick. The teenager who played for Dick Todd became a Hall of Famer. Not because those choices guaranteed success—nothing does—but because they built the muscles that mattered most: the discipline to keep his standards, the resilience to face adversity, and the courage to take ownership.

Your path is waiting. It probably won't be the safe one. It might not even make sense to anyone but you.

To tell you the truth, I still wake up sometimes thinking about all the forks in my life. Each one an echo of that first big choice. Each one asking the same question: Are you going to bet on yourself?

CHAPTER 3

Draft Day Dreams and Nightmares

Getting drafted by the Whalers didn't mean I had a contract. And five minutes to midnight on September 30, I still didn't have one.

The deadline wasn't negotiable. Sign by midnight or go back to junior hockey. Maybe I'd been smart to pack my car that morning; every possession I owned was jammed into my Chevy Cavalier.

That summer, Hartford had placed me with Bob Crispin's family while I played in the preseason and waited to officially sign. Bob was friends with Richard Gordon, the Whalers owner, and he and his family welcomed me into their home. That environment gave me energy, and I was happy being there. Bob and I would have long conversations about business, about life, about hockey. Sometimes we'd watch movies together, like a real family. In fact, Bob and his wife, Kathy, as well as their three kids, truly became like a second family to me—and it has stayed that way, even to this day. I count Bob as one of my greatest mentors.

And the look on his face when I'd loaded my car that morning said everything: *This kid's really going to walk away from this NHL season over money.*

As the clock ticked down, I sat with Pat Verbeek—the Whalers' captain—and watched my agent work the phones from Pat's living room. Our captain understood negotiations, understood leverage, and his house had become our war room. Seven points in seven preseason games, and Hartford was playing hardball.

At 11:55, they blinked.

"Four years, $7 million," my agent said, covering the phone.

The number hit me like a Mike Tyson uppercut. More money than anyone in my family had ever seen. More than established veterans were making. The highest salary on the team for a kid who hadn't played a regular-season game.

The fax machine screamed to life—contracts in the pre-digital age meant actual paper, actual signatures, actual deadlines that could be blown by a paper jam. We signed, faxed, waited. No confirmation. Another fax. Still waiting.

At 12:03 a.m., the phone rang.

"It's registered," my agent said. "You're officially a Hartford Whaler." It was damn good news . . . but the relief lasted about thirty seconds. Then came the weight.

I was eighteen and suddenly making more than guys who'd bled for this team for a decade. I'd become a target. Not just from opponents—from your own teammates wondering why some kid is outearning them. From the media who need controversy. From fans who expect $1.6 million worth of hockey every season.

I called Bob Crispin. "I'm coming home," I said. He just laughed. He knew I'd never actually leave. But he also knew I'd pushed it to the brink, and that said something about what kind of player—what kind of man—I was going to be.

The next morning, I walked into the dressing room knowing everyone knew my number. Their looks said it all: *Prove you're worth it, rookie.*

I felt the pressure, but I can't say that I responded to it well at first. I was good at playing the game how I'd always done it: being an excellent passer, acting as a sponge, and trying to learn everything I could about players' tendencies, going all-in and being aggressive every single play. But while I was working hard in those respects, I was still an eighteen-year-old maturity wise and a little naive.

I did the minimum mandatory workouts; you'd never have found me in the weight room early back in those years. What I didn't know is that the moment you sign that contract, everything changes.

I learned that the hard way at Hartford's 1993 training camp. Seventy-eight guys competing for twenty-three spots, and every single one of them wanted to prove they belonged more than the eighteen-year-old kid, especially a kid who would become the highest-paid player on the team.

I walked into the Hartford Civic Center that smelled like forty years of spilled beer and broken dreams, the ice painted with ads for companies I'd never heard of. This wasn't the Gardens or the Forum. This was hockey's bedroom closet, and I was about to get stuffed in it.

I remember Jay Caufield in the sweaty weight room of training camp. He was a huge ex-football player, and he looked enormous stepping up to the bench press. I don't know if that's because I was still kind of a kid myself or if he really was that huge . . . maybe both. At the bench press, everyone gathered around to see how many reps they could do. With the record set at twenty-eight, Jay took his turn on the bench press and rattled off twenty-nine—just had to one-up, I guess.

That was the vibe of training camp, I learned.

And I was about to learn that was the vibe of professional hockey.

BRAD MCCRIMMON'S ARRIVAL

"Beast" stood in the doorway of my hotel room, all six feet and two hundred pounds of accumulated NHL wisdom, looking like he'd rather be anywhere else.

Brian Burke, GM for the Whalers, had acquired him specifically to "mentor" me. Mentor—hockey code for "make sure this kid doesn't self-destruct."

Brad McCrimmon had started his career in 1979 with the Boston Bruins, picked fifteenth in the first round of the NHL draft in the Big Bad Bruins era. Earned his stripes with the Philadelphia Flyers—the Broad Street Bullies who'd turned violence into virtue. Won a Stanley Cup with Calgary. Mentored a young kid named Nicklas Lidstrom in Detroit who'd become one of the greatest defensemen ever. Beast's style was straightforward: simple, smooth passer, hitting every-thing that moved, clearing the front of the net like he was defusing a bomb, and making forwards pay a price for entering his zone.

Now he was stuck with me. A punk kid making twice his salary who thought he knew everything. We became defense partners, roommates on the road, locker room neighbors—he was 24-7 supervision for Hartford's investment.

His first words to me were, "Be a sponge. You've got a lot to learn."

My response: "Yeah, sure Beast." It became my catchphrase.

He'd explain positioning—"Yeah, sure Beast."

He'd talk about preparation—"Yeah, sure Beast."

He'd stress consistency—"Yeah, sure Beast."

I had all the talent in the world and none of the wisdom to use it properly. Brad saw through the bravado to what I really was: potential without purpose, ability without accountability, a Ferrari engine in a go-kart frame.

"You know what your problem is?" he asked me after a particularly brutal loss where I'd been on ice for three goals against—three times the puck went in our net while I was out there. "You think talent's enough. You think because you can skate backwards faster than most guys can skate forward, you've got it figured out."

He was right. I was coasting on ability, and in the NHL, pure ability alone gets you killed.

I was raw back then. When I was good, I was *really* good, but when I was bad . . . well, you get the picture. Those are the inconsistencies a true pro doesn't have. Beast tried to help me any chance we got—in the hotel room, at dinner. It's not like those were the years you could review tape easily. Back then, not even every game was on TV like it is today. I remember him grabbing salt and pepper shakers and sugar packets to create little rinks on dining tables, peppering me with recap questions and hypothetical scenarios.

"If he goes here," he'd say, "what's your next move?"

"See that?" he'd say, recreating a play where I'd been burned.

"You were thinking about your next move instead of the play in front of you. That half-second of future-thinking? That's why you're out of position. Now Cam Neely, where does he like the puck?"

The list goes on.

Those Hockey 101 sessions were invaluable. Slowly, painfully, the lessons started seeping through my thick skull. Not because I was ready to learn. I was still an arrogant kid who thought he had the answers. It was because Beast never stopped teaching. He taught me strategy, how to have a hockey mind. There was no moment that wasn't a teaching moment, no time of day when it wasn't time for a lesson.

"Consistency is the hallmark of a true pro," he'd say. "Now, how do you become consistent?"

This idea of consistency—one that ultimately boils down to standards—would come back to haunt me later. Because I had none. I prepared when I felt like it, worked hard when motivated, focused when the mood struck. Everything was feeling-based, emotion-driven, as reliable as Hartford weather.

This was Beast's fifteenth year in the NHL. He'd seen plenty of can't-miss prospects miss spectacularly. He knew talent was just the entry fee. The real price of admission was what you did every single day when no one was watching, when you didn't feel like it, when the season ground you down to dust.

But I wasn't ready to hear it. Not yet. I had to fall first. Had to hit bottom. Had to have fifteen thousand people booing me in my own building before I'd finally understand what Brad had been trying to teach me:

In the NHL, as in much of life, talent opens doors. Standards keep them open.

In the NHL, as in much of life, talent opens doors. Standards keep them open.

THE SLIDE BEGINS

By January, the novelty had worn off and reality had set in like a New England winter—brutal, unforgiving, and longer than you ever imagined possible.

We were almost dead last in the league. (Thank God for the Ottawa Senators!) Twenty-six teams, and we were twenty-fifth. Every night felt like skating uphill in quicksand. The losing infected everything—practice, the room, the city. You could feel it in the air at the Hartford Civic Center, this toxic mix of disappointment and resignation.

The team was unraveling—and so was I. The mistakes started compounding. My mistakes. A bad pinch—stepping up too far to keep the puck in—leading to an odd-man rush the other way. A lazy clear resulting in a goal. Lost coverage on my man because I was thinking about everything except hockey. Each mistake felt magnified because of my contract—the expectations that came with being the team's highest-paid player—and because Hartford needed someone to blame for being terrible. And I was giving them exactly what they wanted.

The rink had always been my sanctuary, and by that point, it, too, had become a disaster. By March, we were still in second to last place and out of the playoffs by a mile. I was getting crushed by crowds every night and felt things slipping. To top it all off, I was bored out of my mind.

Then came Buffalo. The Sabres were jockeying with the Boston Bruins for the top seed in the Eastern Conference while we were stuck at the bottom. At only nineteen, most nights I couldn't go out with the rest of the team like I wanted to. Looking back, I can see I was lonely and depressed. A couple of nights before the Sabres game, our entire team went to a bar—coaches included. I was underage, but it didn't matter; we were just standing around and chatting when a bouncer grabbed our captain's beer. We protested. More bouncers came.

"Just let us walk out," I said. "We're not here to fight."

They didn't listen. By the end of the night, seven of us plus one random guy—shoutout to Jerry Brown—had gotten arrested. They carted us around in the back of the cop car like some sideshow. We slept it off in jail, and as a naive kid, I didn't think much of it until we were released and saw all of the press. In reaction mode, I pulled my jacket up over my face, and someone snapped a photo that would follow me around for years. Then the media firestorm came: *Does Chris have a drinking problem? Is he too immature for the NHL? Does he understand how to be a pro?* The truth? I was miserable—the losing, being booed every night, feeling stuck in the city. I just needed a break.

A couple of weeks later, after our season ended in April, I drove out to Bowling Green State University to visit my brother. We got into an argument, so my brilliant ass decided to drive to Toronto to try to visit a friend. Then the flashing lights fell in behind me. DUI. Another mistake, another byproduct of my lack of standards.

The season ended with us second to last, even behind a couple of expansion teams, and I still had to face the DUI. I pled "no contest" and had to attend counseling, which was held inside a jail—three days in at nineteen years old.

In Buffalo, I'd been at the wrong place at the wrong time. But I'm not sure I would've done anything differently if I had to do it all over again. I was out with my teammates and we didn't do anything wrong. It was definitely an eye-opening experience, though, and something that would test me for years. It was a shitty ending to an even shittier year.

That summer, I was back at it—training hard, all-in. I came into camp in great shape . . . then came the lockout of 1994. Players scattered: Some of the bigger names went to Europe after a month of no hockey, while others stayed. I wanted to go to the minors, but the National Hockey League Players' Association (NHLPA) said no at that time. I couldn't go back to junior, either. Just stuck.

In those three months, I didn't work out all that much and had myself a real good time. To me it felt like that was my opportunity to get the full college experience that I was missing. When the lockout ended in early January and training camp started again, I was in terrible shape—getting outskated, getting winded easily. To make it worse, I separated my shoulder in the fifth game of the lockout-shortened season.

At twenty years old, I didn't yet understand that people's jobs were on the line every time I stepped on the ice—coaches, teammates, management, the training staff. I was focused on myself. Now, I can see my own immaturity and unprofessionalism—but that took years to understand.

At the time, the slide felt inevitable, like gravity had taken over and I was just along for the ride. Each game got harder. Each mistake got bigger. Each boo got louder. I'd gone from can't-miss prospect to can't-watch disaster in less than a season.

Even then, I had raw talent. That was undeniable. I was even told by our GM at our exit meetings in the spring of '95 that I was Hartford's "franchise player." This gave me hope. Maybe I still had a future here.

Then, the bomb dropped: I'd been traded. And not for just anyone. St. Louis gave up one of the league's biggest stars—their leader and fan favorite, Brendan Shanahan—to get me.

I never saw it coming.

The headlines were brutal. Blues fans wanted blood. Whalers fans seemed ecstatic about what they were getting. And I was a kid trying to figure out how I'd live up to a deal like that.

ROCK BOTTOM WITH THE BLUES

Mike Keenan, the Blues' hard-edged head coach and general manager, had been the head coach of Peterborough many years before I played there, and Dick Todd had been his trainer. When I joined the Petes, Dick Todd was my coach. Small world, hockey.

Beyond the connection, Keenan had a reputation. He was known for picking players with star potential, breaking them down, then building them back up—but better. "Iron Mike," they called him—and I was about to find out why.

While the coaching staff might have been happy about the trade, the rest of St. Louis didn't exactly share that sentiment. Fans were furious. They'd just lost Brendan Shanahan in exchange for me—an unproven defenseman who was thinking about everything except reacting to what was on the ice.

What if they boo me again? What if I get yelled at? What if I miss this play?

I was so weak-minded that everything bothered me. *When are these people going to leave me alone, and why are they always picking on just me?*

All that goes into good hockey—preparation, consistency, how you practice, how you fuel yourself, the standards that would come later—I was doing none of those things. I could almost hear Beast's voice in my head from a few years before. I still wasn't ready to listen. I just wanted to show up and play. Back then, the fans were immaterial to me.

You want to be entertained? I thought. *I will entertain you with how I play. I'm not going to throw pucks into the stands during a game or smile for pictures.*

For that reason and probably a lot of others, the boos started immediately. Not scattered discontent— orchestrated hatred. I was in Coach Keenan's office before every game, in between periods, after every game.

It would go something like this: My defense partner pinches, gambling to keep the puck in, and it doesn't work. I'm facing a three-on-one. I dive to block. They tic-tac-toe around me. Goal.

"Chris! Come here," Keenan would yell.

Goddammit, I'd think, sitting in my stall. *Not again.* I'd sulk to his office to get yelled at.

"What the hell are you doing? Why did you slide?"

Why the hell did he pinch? I'd think to myself. That was the victimhood mindset I was in. Blame the other guy. Feel sorry for myself.

I struggled mightily under the pressure of the trade and expectations, going deeper and deeper into a hole. The mental side of things was crushing the physical side of my game, and I was questioning every decision in a way that made me lose the ability to react to the situation in front of me on the ice.

The pressure was building, the depression deepening, the booing becoming louder. Going out in public was becoming an issue because fans would recognize me and cut glances or hurl comments my way. I could barely stand the negativity.

Still, it wasn't all bad. I knew Mike saw something in me at the end of the day—something enough to trade a star player to get me. But the situation was eating away at my soul.

One day, on a team flight midway through my first year with the Blues, Coach Keenan waved me up to the front of the plane. While he hasn't always been known for his heart, he's a good man. He could see I was dying a slow death by how I was playing and how the fans were treating me. To top it all off, I know he was personally taking shit from the fans, media, and probably even people inside the organization for making the trade and bringing me there.

"Here," he said, handing me a slip of paper. "It's a sports psychologist, good guy. I use him too. Give him a call."

Turns out, rock bottom has a basement.

KEENAN'S SURPRISE

"What are your standards?"

Dr. Miller sat across from me in his tiny office, legal pad in hand, waiting for an answer I didn't have. He was older than I expected, maybe sixty, with the kind of calm that made you want to either trust him completely or punch him in the face.

I'd had three years of reporters asking if I was a bust, three years of wondering if they were right. I answered, "My what?"

"Standards. The non-negotiables you live by. The baseline below which you won't drop regardless of circumstances."

I stared at him. Standards? I had talent. I had size. I had an incredible contract. What the hell were standards?

"I work hard," I tried.

"Sometimes?"

"Yeah, I mean—most of the time."

"So working hard is negotiable. What else?"

"I want to win."

"Everyone wants to win. What do you do to ensure it?"

"I . . . prepare."

"When you feel like it?"

This went on for twenty minutes. Every answer I gave, he gently pulled apart to show it wasn't a standard—it was a preference, a sometimes-thing, a when-I-feel-like-it approach to professional sports.

"Chris," he finally said, putting down his pen. "You're trying to build an elite career on a foundation of feelings. When you feel good, you play well. When you feel bad, you play poorly. Your entire professional existence depends on what mood you wake up in. At some point, you're going to run out of opportunities."

The truth hit like a body check.

My throat went dry. *Out of opportunities.* Beast's words from a couple years before in Hartford, now coming in a different room, from a different mouth.

"So what do I do?"

"We start with three standards. Not thirty. Not ten. Three. Simple, specific, daily non-negotiables that you execute regardless of how you feel, how the team's doing, or how many people boo."

He slid the legal pad across the coffee table.

"Write them down. And understand—these aren't goals. Goals are things you work toward. Standards are things you never drop below. Ever."

I stared at the blank page. Three things. How hard could that be?

"I don't know where to start," I said.

"Work out every day?" Dr. Miller questioned.

"Define 'work out.' Twenty push-ups counts as working out."

"Yes."

"Be the hardest worker in the room," I said and wrote it down.

"Fuel my body with appropriate nutrition." I added it to the list.

"Good. There's two. Give me one more."

The last one took longer. While the first two addressed the physical, the mental side was less clear. I had to address the booing, the benching, the spiral— that was internal.

"No more victimhood mentality," I said. On the page, I wrote, "No more excuses. Take ownership."

Dr. Miller studied the list. "These aren't revolutionary. Any junior player could write these. The difference is whether you'll actually do them when you're tired, angry, frustrated, or being booed by your home crowd."

"I will."

"We'll see. Because here's the hard truth—standards without execution are just wishes. And right now, Chris, you're wishing your way through the NHL."

Standards without execution are just wishes.

He was right. I'd been hoping things would get better, hoping the booing would stop, hoping my game would magically return. *Hope isn't a strategy*, I thought. *Standards might be.*

The paper in my hand felt heavier than my equipment bag. Three lines of text that would either save me or serve as my NHL obituary. I read it again.

1. *Be the hardest worker in the room.*
2. *Fuel my body with appropriate nutrition.*
3. *No more excuses. Take ownership.*

After I met with Dr. Miller, the Blues traded for Wayne Gretzky. In Gretz, the fans had someone else to focus on, someone else to celebrate or skewer, depending on last night's game. (Even though this was the sixteenth of his twenty years in the NHL, he was still the Great One.) Those eyes turning away from me gave me some breathing room, which meant I had time to implement my standards.

And that made all the difference.

ACT II

Trials and Transformation

CHAPTER 4

Standards and Adversity

Life is all about peaks and valleys, but after that meeting with Dr. Miller, I was on the upswing.

And then, my heart stopped.

No, I mean literally.

Because that's the thing about momentum: Life has a way of testing whether you really mean it.

May 10, 1998. Game 2 against Detroit. Second round of the NHL playoffs. We were down 1–0 in the series. I'd been living by my standards for almost two years, and they were working. In fact, I'd just been announced as a Norris Trophy nominee (for the league's top-defenseman award) and was finally playing like that six-year, $16.35 million deal was a bargain.

In that playoff game, as we were killing a penalty—down a man, trying to survive Detroit's power play—I did what every defenseman does in that situation: sacrificed. Penalty kills are about blocking shots by throwing your body in front of pucks. And that's exactly what happened. I dropped into the lane and a slapshot put a puck in my chest. Nothing special, right? I'd blocked a thousand shots. But this time, the puck came up at just the wrong angle and caught me right in the heart.

It felt like the wind had been knocked out of me and I noticed a stinging burn. In my mind, I went to corral the puck to get a whistle for a faceoff so that I could get to the bench nearby. I did not want to lie there on the ice, as we were in Detroit and I knew the boobirds would be chirping in short order.

The next thing I knew, I was staring up at the banners hanging from the rafters in Joe Louis Arena, wondering why a crowd of trainers, players, and doctors were hovering over me. It took me a second to register where I was and what was going on. I saw Ray Barile, our head medical trainer, and started talking to him. (I still remember Ray looking so relieved that I had come to.) My parents were at that game, and I immediately told the trainers to get a hold of them and let them know I was okay.

Still flat on my back on the ice, I responded to the trainers and doctors as they put me on a stretcher and carried me out to the waiting ambulance. During the ride to the hospital, the medical team tried to fill me in about what had happened, but I felt disoriented. Even as I was wheeled into a hospital room, I didn't fully comprehend everything. I only knew there were cords all over me and beeping sounds coming from all around, with doctors and nurses coming and going.

Twenty-three years old, in peak physical condition, and I found myself lying in a hospital bed wondering if my career—hell, my life—was over. A nurse came in every hour to check if I was still alive. That's not an exaggeration. That was literally her job: make sure Chris Pronger's heart keeps beating. (The monitors were not as advanced and automated as they are today.)

I remember Brendan Shanahan—that player I was traded for a few years earlier who was now the star of our rival Red Wings—came to visit me in the hospital unexpectedly after the game. I admit that it was a little awkward, especially since I hadn't spoken to him since the trade. But it was also thoughtful of him, and it meant a lot.

You want to talk about perspective? Try having your heart stop. But I had grit and perseverance. I didn't care how many tubes were in me; I wanted to get back on the ice. If there's one thing I learned over all the years of being booed, it's to leave it all out there. No regrets. And I was unwilling to accept the consequences of not playing, whatever those may be.

I finally fell asleep that night, but as soon as I woke the next morning, I wanted to figure out what had happened, why it happened, and what Game 3 might look like for me. I flew home later that morning and went to see a heart specialist in St. Louis, Dr. Cole. She began a battery of tests, ultimately using words like "commotio cordis" and "cardiac event." Fancy medical terms for "the puck stopped your heart, and we weren't so sure it was going to start properly again. But it looks like it was a freak accident."

I never doubted I'd be back, cleared or not. By Game 3 of the playoff series, just two days later, I was on the ice again. I vividly recall lining up against Joey Kocur, one of Detroit's tough guys I'd been jawing with all series. He leaned in close during the faceoff and said, his voice low, "Glad you're okay."

Right after, we were on the ice, trying to wreck each other again. That moment, the moment with Brendan, the concern from my team and the fans . . . that's what brings the humanity to the game. The magnitude of certain moments are above the competition. While I didn't expect any of it, I appreciated it more than I probably let on.

Here's what I learned flat on my back in that hospital: Standards aren't just for when things are going well. They're for when life hits you in the chest—literally or figuratively—and tries to stop your heart. They're what you hold on to when everything else falls apart.

Here's what I learned flat on my back in that hospital: Standards aren't just for when things are going well. They're for when life hits you in the chest—literally or figuratively— and tries to stop your heart. They're what you hold on to when everything else falls apart.

Before my heart stopped, I'd been hearing my name mentioned—for the first time in my career—with the best defensemen in the league. Not as potential but as reality. The same writers who'd crucified me were now voting for me as a Norris Trophy nominee.

"How does it feel?" a reporter asked after practice. "Three years ago, this building wanted you traded. Now you're up for the Norris."

I thought back to the question that had changed everything: *What are your standards?*

"Three years ago, I didn't deserve their respect," I said. "Now I do. That's the only difference that matters."

But the Norris nomination was just external validation of an internal transformation. The real victory was who I'd become as those three statements I wrote down in Dr. Miller's office had come to fruition:

- The guy who did the bare minimum now loved to work out. > *Be the hardest worker in the room.*

- The guy who made excuses for everything now owned every mistake. > *No more excuses. Take ownership.*
- The guy who floated on talent now outworked everyone through preparation. > *Fuel my body with appropriate nutrition.* (And I'd added another standard: *Choose discipline over comfort.*)

My teammates noticed. Management noticed. Hell, even the fans noticed. They could see it in my discipline, my professionalism, my physical shape. It's like the standards had rewired my brain. Every decision now filtered through them: *Does this action align with my standards? If not, why am I doing it?*

It wasn't about perfection. I still made mistakes. Still had bad games. Still got beat sometimes. But now I had a framework for improvement. A bad game wasn't a disaster . . . it was data. A mistake wasn't failure . . . it was feedback.

FROM BOOED TO NORRIS: THE FIVE-YEAR TRANSFORMATION

"You came back different," Beast told me that summer. We'd become friends by then, the mentorship finally taking hold after years of my resistance.

"Different how?"

"Hungrier. Like you realized something the rest of us are still figuring out."

I was back on the ice, and Beast had noticed my change. He was right. When you've felt your heart stop, every heartbeat after is a gift. Every workout, every game, every opportunity to improve—they're not obligations anymore. They're privileges.

That cardiac event could have ended everything. Instead, it crystallized everything. The standards I'd been living with suddenly had deeper meaning. They weren't just about becoming a better hockey player. They were about becoming someone who deserved the second chance I'd been given.

By 1997–1998, my fifth year as a pro, I'd spent two years living with standards. That's 900-plus days of no excuses, 900-plus days of choosing discipline over comfort.

The transformation was complete. Or so I thought.

Here's the thing: Standards don't make you invincible. They just prepare you for whatever comes next, including adversity.

A BANNER YEAR TO REMEMBER—AND FORGET

During the 1998–1999 season, I hurt my ankle and had to do what I hated: watch the game I loved instead of playing it. My mentor and fellow defenseman, Al

MacInnis, won the Norris that year. He'd played spectacularly in my absence. I had two years left on my contract, and my agent and I asked the Blues if they were
interested in working on an extension. The response I
got amounted to something like, "Nope, not until you
go show us what kind of player you can be."

After missing time during the season to heal, I was
entering the summer as healthy as I had ever been and
started training immediately. Through Al, I also met
my new trainer, Charles Poliquin—a legend who set
the gold standard for athletic training. His regimen was
strict: a high-protein diet, an incredibly detailed workout
schedule . . . the works. He completely changed how I
ate, how I trained.

Management wanted to see me play, and I was going
to give them a hell of a show. And I did.

Adversity? I faced it.

Ownership? I took it.

Standards? I had them.

The 1999–2000 season was one for the ages. I won
the Norris as best defenseman and the Hart Trophy as
League MVP.

I also met Lauren, my future wife, in early January
when she came over to my house with a group of friends.
I wasn't looking for anything serious, but as soon as I
saw her, I knew it was game over. Sure enough, we got

married the following year and have been by each other's sides ever since.

With things looking up on and off the ice, I skated into the playoffs with my head held high . . . and then we shit the bed in the first round. I was so pissed off that we lost—and in an embarrassing fashion—that frankly I had a hard time enjoying my individual trophies. I was grateful for the honors, sure, but what good is an MVP if your team flames out in April? We'd fallen apart when we needed to rise above the adversity. Watching the New Jersey Devils skate around with the Cup while we sat at home was torture.

We should've been there, or at least been in the conversation, I thought.

Losing did not sit well with me back then, and I was applying too much pressure on myself. Whispers of, "Oh, you just can't win with this guy," floated around the media and the hockey world. What good did it do to have an incredible year if your team didn't get it done in the end?

That's the thing about hockey: It's the ultimate team sport, and I mean it really takes the whole team. It's not like in other sports where one person has the ball and takes the glory or the pain. In hockey, if the team doesn't win, the captains and star players usually get the blame regardless. There were countless times when my teammates didn't like how I went so hard in practice, never letting up, challenging them and challenging myself. That's because I needed them to play to the best of their abilities. I was trying to bring out the best in them. If I didn't, my ass was on the line.

This evolution was huge for me. Back in Hartford and my early St. Louis days, I couldn't understand why the veteran players rode me so hard. But as I became the one in the spotlight, I could see it clearly: So much depends on winning—not just your job, but the jobs of your teammates, the coaching staff, you name it. It took me a while to take it seriously because I was still a kid when I got started in the NHL, but by the time 2000 rolled around, I was doing nothing but taking it seriously.

After that disappointing ending to the season, I had one year left on my contract with the Blues. In late October, I again met with my agent, Pat Morris, and GM, Larry Pleau.

"You told me to go show you, and I showed you," I told Larry.

"Yes, you did," he agreed. "We'll take that deal you offered before last season."

I laughed.

"That was before," I said. "I just won the MVP. I know what I'm worth. You know what I'm worth. What's the number now? What are we arguing about here? You can either pay me what I am worth or trade me, and you won't trade me. So where does that leave us? I'm happy here. I want to play here. I want to win here."

By November of 2000, I'd signed a contract to be one of the league's highest-paid defenseman: a three-year, $29.5 million deal with a $1 million signing bonus. Not bad for a kid from Dryden, eh?

THE LONG AND WINDING ROAD

The year after I won the Hart, my knee was bothering me halfway through the year. In consultation with the Blues, I decided to get knee surgery at the All-Star break so that it wouldn't bother me during the playoffs. My second game back from rehabbing my knee, I was coming out of the penalty box and was inadvertently hit with a slap shot from a teammate trying to ice the puck. The result? What's called a night-stick fracture. The puck hit directly on my forearm and shattered my wrist. To facilitate the healing process (which would allow me to get back in time for the playoffs), I had a plate put in my forearm, but that injury would go on to bother me for the next three seasons.

I returned at the start of the playoffs with my left wrist incredibly weak. We do what we can in order to play, but I was not able to play up to my standard. Still, we advanced to the Western Conference Finals before bowing out to the Colorado Avalanche, who went on to win the Stanley Cup. Over the summer, I trained in preparation for coming back at 100 percent, but my wrist, which led to elbow and shoulder issues, was compromised. I played the 2001–2002 season in a lot of pain, struggling to get healthy.

During our second-round playoff series against Detroit (which we lost, 4–1), I tore my ACL. As I was learning what that rehab process was going to look like, I also decided to have wrist surgery—then spent that summer trying to rehab both my knee and my wrist. The knee was coming along fine, but my wrist was still posing a serious problem. As camp approached, I had lost range of motion in my wrist and was unable to hold my stick properly.

To find a solution, I went on a "doctor roadshow" to meet with medical specialists who could fix the problem. I saw three: one in Toronto, one in Baltimore, and one in St. Louis. The doctor in Toronto thought I would/ should be able to return in three weeks after the surgery he advised. That seemed a little aggressive to us. The St. Louis doc said I would miss another season. That seemed a little long. Then I met with Dr. Tom Graham.

Immediately, I responded to his bedside manner and his understanding of the surgery. He knew what would be necessary to fix the problem, and I felt comfortable right from the outset. Dr. Graham used an approach called the Darrach Procedure—basically, cutting out one inch of my wrist to alleviate the pain and allow joint mobility. It was an aggressive surgery, but a necessary one if I was going to get back to 100 percent. He would also remove the titanium plate that was becoming troublesome.

To me, it was never worth playing if I couldn't be at 100 percent because that wouldn't be up to my standard, so it was a risk I was willing to take. To my knowledge, I would be the first professional athlete to undergo that particular procedure, and you know what? It worked. The moment I got out of surgery, I felt relief. No pressure in my arm, no pain in my wrist. The surgery was a success. I came back in time for the 2002–2003 playoffs and then played a full season the following year—I'd proven I could stay healthy. After that season, I knew I was back . . . but we were about to embark on yet another NHL lockout that lasted the whole next season.

When I knew the league was going to give me the green light to play, I also knew it was time for me to leave St. Louis. There were a lot of rumors swirling around about where I might be traded. Ultimately, I was traded to Edmonton, an option the Oilers had kept very quiet. In fact, Lauren and I had not heard of them as an option during the course of the post-lockout trade rumors.

I agreed to a five-year deal with Edmonton in one of the biggest negotiation fuckups of my career. (I'll share more about that in chapter 6.) Midway through my first year, I told my agent I would need to be traded at the end of the first season. The months that followed tested every standard I had. I played knowing I'd be leaving. Kept my mouth shut. Gave maximum effort every night and day. Helped to lead the team to the Stanley Cup Finals.

June 19, 2006. Game 7 was a Holy Grail of a game—the one every player chases, the game that could deliver immortality or heartbreak. And with just over a minute left, we went down 3–1 after Justin Williams scored into our empty net.

I stood at the blue line, stick on the ice, watching that last faceoff. My foot was broken, my back was wrecked, and my elbow was throbbing as the fluid built up. The floating bone chips in my knee made skating feel like grinding metal on metal.

But the pain was just noise. All that mattered was the clock—sixty-one seconds between me and the end of everything we'd fought for.

The horn sounded.

Just like that, it was over.

I dropped my stick right there on the ice. Didn't even bend to pick it up. The Carolina crowd—nineteen thousand strong—went ballistic. Confetti rained down. The crowd was deafening, and the sight of the Hurricanes celebrating at their end of the ice made me want to puke.

Game 822 of my career. Game 822 without a Stanley Cup.

The skate to our bench was miserable. My teammates sat slumped on the bench, some staring at the ice, others watching Carolina celebrate what should've been ours. The traditional post-series handshakes with the winners were heartfelt but wrenching.

In the tunnel, nobody spoke. What was there to say? We'd given everything. Bled for each other. Sacrificed our bodies night after night. And for what?

The locker room door closed behind us with a finality that made my chest tighten. That's when the real inventory began. Guys started peeling off equipment, revealing the hidden toll of our journey. As with all playoff runs of this magnitude, the injuries started to come into the public eye. We had a number of players who needed surgery post-playoffs.

I sat in my stall, unlacing my skates for what I knew would be my last time in an Oilers jersey. My hands shook—not from emotion, but from sheer exhaustion. We'd played twenty-four playoff games. I'd averaged over 30:57 minutes of ice time per game—a total of 743 minutes. Twelve-plus hours. My body felt like it had been fed through a wood chipper.

All for nothing. We go home without the trophy that we should have won.

TRAINWRECK

We'd lost Game 7 on a Monday. The next day, we flew back and I went to a house I'd already packed up. Most of it was rental furniture anyway. The draft was scheduled for Saturday in Vancouver, where Kevin Lowe, Edmonton's GM, was going to have to trade his star player.

Lauren was already back at our home in St. Louis when the news of my trade request had started to leak. Even though I'd known I'd be leaving, I'd played to win, just like I always did. But not everybody saw it like that. Some fans made up lies . . . they loved me at first, but then they loved to hate me because they felt like I'd rejected them, essentially. I was prepared for the backlash but not the slander.

I did my exit interviews and got my ass on a plane out of there.

C'est la vie, I suppose. I'm a big boy.

COLORADO COLLAPSE

Two weeks later, I couldn't get out of bed.

Lauren and I had flown to Colorado to visit dear friends, to decompress, to get away from Edmonton and the weight of what we'd lost. She'd suggested hiking, maybe some golf. Normal-people stuff. Stuff you do when your body hasn't been systematically destroyed over two months of playoff hockey.

I made it two blocks down the street in Beaver Creek before my knee locked completely. Not the usual stiffness—this was like someone had poured concrete into the joint. I grabbed a lamppost to keep from falling.

"Chris?" Lauren's voice sounded far away, even though she was right beside me.

"I'm fine," I lied, trying to put weight on the leg. Nothing. The knee wouldn't bend at all.

She helped me limp to a bench. Tourists walked by, probably wondering why this giant was sweating bullets on a seventy-degree day. They had no idea that under my jeans, my knee looked like a grapefruit—swollen and angry.

That night at dinner, my elbow swelled so badly I couldn't bend it to cut my steak. The waiter must've thought I was drunk, watching me try to eat left-handed, dropping food like a toddler.

"Maybe we should go home," Lauren suggested gently.

"I'm fine," I said again.

But I wasn't fine. None of us were. You don't play through what we'd played through and just bounce back. The adrenaline that had kept us upright for two months was gone, and our bodies were presenting the bill.

I thought about my teammates, scattered across the continent, probably dealing with their own collapses. We'd asked our bodies to do the impossible, and for 106 games (regular season and playoffs), they'd answered. But bodies keep score, even when your mind tries to forget.

CHAPTER 5

Raising the Cup

In all of the Edmonton backlash, Brian Burke—the GM who'd been part of drafting me in Hartford all those years ago, and who was now running Anaheim—brings me in once again. New team. New colors. New chance.

I walk into the Anaheim Ducks' practice facility, and one of the first guys I spot is Teemu Selänne. *For the last decade*, I think, *I've been working this guy over every chance I got. Slashes, cross-checks, the occasional face wash. The usual defenseman hospitality. Now I'm supposed to be protecting him?*

I walk over. "Teemu."

He looks at me, and I can see him thinking about all the shit I'd put him through. Then he breaks into that famous grin.

"Prongs! Finally, you stop hitting me and start hitting other people!"

We hug it out. Just like that. Because that's hockey. Yesterday's enemy is today's teammate, and everybody understands the game. This was a big deal for everyone to see.

Brian Burke had assembled something special here. Niedermayer and me on the back end—along with our gritty D partners, Francois Beauchemin and Sean O'Donnell—was probably the best defensive pairing in the league. Selänne still scoring at age thirty-six. Young guns like Getzlaf and Perry ready to explode on the NHL scene. A goalie in Jean-Sebastien Giguere who could steal any game. An incredible checking line of Moen-Påhlsson-Niedermayer. And a hard-nosed fourth line that could match any team's ferocity.

But talent doesn't win championships. I'd learned that the hard way. Culture wins championships. Standards win championships.

But talent doesn't win championships.
I'd learned that the hard way.
Culture wins championships.
Standards win championships.

These guys had lost Game 7 to New Jersey back in '03. They'd been bounced by Edmonton—my Edmonton— just months ago in the 2006 playoffs. They weren't satisfied with being good.

They wanted to be great.

Having been on the other side in Edmonton playing against Anaheim in the Western Conference Final the year before, I knew that the depth of the team, with the addition of myself, made it Stanley Cup or bust. Every player on that team, every coach, every trainer, every member of management and ownership knew . . . this team had been put together specifically to win. Our word for that season was BELIEVE, and everyone believed we'd been brought together to accomplish something special.

This was a team that understood what I'd learned losing Game 822 with the Oilers: Effort isn't enough. Good isn't great. And if you want to be a champion, you better be willing to do whatever it takes.

GAME 911, THE CUP CLINCHER

June 6, 2007. Ottawa is in our barn. Game 5 of the Stanley Cup Finals.

We're up 3–1 in the series, leading 5–2 early into the third period. The Cup is in the building. After 911 regular season and playoff games, I'm less than twenty minutes away from everything I'd sacrificed for.

But I'm not thinking about that. I'm thinking about one thing: *Don't let up. Don't give them life. Don't become another Game 7 story.*

With five minutes left, our D coach, Dave Farrish, taps me on the shoulder. "Prongs, you're up."

I hop over the boards, and the noise hits me like a wave . . . 17,500 Anaheim fans are going berserk with what is about to transpire. Our bench knows it too. Hell, everyone in the building knows it except for one group: the champions. Champions play to the final buzzer.

When Ottawa wins a faceoff in our zone, we see their desperation—crashing the net, throwing everything at Giguere. A scramble in front. Then the puck squirts to Daniel Alfredsson in the slot. I slide over, get my stick on his shot, and deflect the puck wide.

Two minutes left. "Stay calm!" I'm yelling at our young guys. "Do your job!"

The final minute ticks down. I'm on the ice—where I was meant to be. Where I'd earned the right to be through 911 games of punishment and persistence.

Ten seconds left.

The puck slides into the corner. I chase it down and look up the ice. No highlight-reel play. No risk. I hold the puck and wait.

Three. Two. One.

The horn blares.

The weight of everything—Hartford's boos, St. Louis's disappointments, Edmonton's Game 7, every surgery and setback—lifted all at once.

My team mobs each other celebrating. And the media later makes up their own stories about why I stuck the puck in my hockey pants. I had my reasons. I had separated my shoulder in the first period of the game, so I wasn't in a position to get in the middle of the mob. But I'd picked up that puck for Brian Burke. The man who drafted me in Hartford all those years ago when I just had potential. Who gave me another shot when Edmonton soured. Who had put this incredible team together. Who *believed*.

People gave me heat for that, saying I was selfish because I didn't celebrate with my teammates and had grabbed the puck.

They didn't understand. Without Burke believing in me—twice—I'm not holding that Cup. Sometimes you have to acknowledge the people who bet on you when others wouldn't.

BEAST'S ONE-THOUSANDTH-GAME MESSAGE

February 20, 2009. We're in Detroit, and their assistant coach—Brad McCrimmon, Beast, my old roommate from Hartford—had just watched me play my one thousandth career game. He'd seen my first game, and now, he'd seen my thousandth.

He came into the locker room right after the buzzer sounded with an envelope for me. The note inside meant so much.

Feb 20, 2009

Chris,

Congratulations on playing your 1000th game in the NHL, it is amazing how time flies! It seems like yesterday I was part of your 1st game now here we are and I get to part of your 1000th game. It was good to see your Mom and Dad, as we know none of us get here with out love and support from our families and friends.

When I think of you I remember a lot of things like the first lesson you learned in Montreal, last minute, and the puck did not get out.....and ended up in our net. You cleaned yourself off and absorbed the lesson. This trait of being a true student of the game and respecting the game has served you well, as I have been witness to a player who knows the game, the players and in always prepared for battle, a true warrior.

More than being a student you have been a true professional. You have reached a level of play few achieve and that is a tribute to you. The level of commitment and sacrifice required to play 1000 games are known by a small number indeed, and as time passes you will understand this.

It was my pleasure to be your teammate but more than that it is our friendship that I hold close because that is for ever.

Sincerely

Brad McCrimmon

We shook hands. Teacher and student. Mentor and mentee. Two guys who'd traveled very different roads to the same destination: one thousand games of earned wisdom.

It made me emotional. And Beast was right. When I was eighteen, living like I'd already made it, he tried to save me from myself. Every day.

"The game will humble you," he'd say.

"Standards matter," he'd say.

"You can't cheat the process," he'd say.

"Yeah, sure Beast," I'd respond, almost always dismissively.

Now here I was, a thousand games in, finally understanding every word he'd tried to teach me. The irony wasn't lost on me. He was celebrating from the bench while I was still playing, but we both knew the truth: He'd figured it out way before I did.

THE 2010 OLYMPICS: COMING HOME

Vancouver, February 28, 2010. Gold medal at stake. Canada versus USA. On home soil.

This wasn't just any Olympics. This was a chance to rewrite history.

I'd been part of the disaster in Nagano in '98 when we finished fourth. Part of the redemption in 2002 when we won gold in Salt Lake City. Part of the catastrophe in 2006 in Torino when we finished seventh. Three

Olympics, three completely different experiences. But this one? This felt unique from the moment we arrived.

The pressure was otherworldly. Canada hadn't won Olympic gold on home soil since 1952. The entire country was watching. Expecting. Demanding.

Pressure only crushes those without standards. And this team? We had standards in spades.

Steve Yzerman had put together a roster that prioritized one thing: character. Sure, we had skill—Crosby, Iginla, Thornton, Getzlaf, Perry (my Anaheim boys). But more importantly, we had guys who understood their roles and embraced them.

Take Rick Nash. Fifty-goal scorer in Columbus. On our team? Fourth-line checker and penalty killer. And he attacked that role like his life depended on it.

That's what 2006 had been missing. Guys worried about ice time, about their roles, about their egos. In Vancouver, ego was checked at the door. We had one mission: Win gold for Canada. Everything else was secondary.

The gold-medal game itself was everything you'd want. Back and forth. Canada up, 2–0. The US battling back. Zach Parise tying it for them with twenty-four seconds left in regulation. The entirety of our country (and theirs) holding its breath.

Then, 7:40 into overtime. Crosby to Iginla. Iginla back to Crosby. The golden goal.

As the building exploded and my teammates piled on Sid, I stood at the blue line for a second, taking it in. Four Olympics. Two golds. Bookends to a journey that started with me as a twenty-three-year-old who was learning he didn't know everything and ended with me at thirty-five, finally understanding what Brad McCrimmon had tried to teach me all those years ago: Excellence isn't about talent. It's about standards. It's about sacrifice. It's about being willing to do whatever your team needs, whenever they need it.

Excellence isn't about talent.
It's about standards.

That 2010 victory was our country's twenty-fifth gold medal at those Games—the most ever by Canada at a Winter Olympics. We'd saved the best for last. The men's hockey gold medal, in Canada, in overtime, against the Americans.

You couldn't script it better.

Standing on that blue line, watching my teammates celebrate, I thought about the road that led here. Every trade. Every injury. Every failure. They weren't detours— they were the route. You can't appreciate the summit if you haven't crawled through the valleys.

That's what I'd learned in 911 games, then one thousand, then four Olympics: The destination matters, but the journey and the scars along that path are what make you.

REFLECTIONS ON STANDARDS, ADVERSITY, OWNERSHIP—AND SUCCESS

Looking back at that run from 2006 to 2010—from forcing a trade out of Edmonton to winning the Stanley Cup to Olympic gold—I can trace it all back to three things: standards, adversity, and ownership.

Not talent. I'd had talent in Hartford and flamed out. Not opportunity. I'd had opportunity in Edmonton and played my ass off under horrendous conditions. I finally had non-negotiable standards. I embraced adversity as the iron that sharpened me, and I took ownership instead of hiding behind excuses.

Standards mean showing up every single day and doing the work, especially when you don't feel like it.

Standards mean showing up every single day and doing the work, especially when you don't feel like it.

In Anaheim, my standards were simple:

- Leave it all on the ice. No regrets.
- Prepare and put the work in. Treat every practice like a game.
- Hold teammates accountable, but hold myself to a higher standard first.
- No excuses. Ever.

Adversity was unavoidable: injuries, trades, losses, the noise of critics. Instead of being setbacks, they tested my standards. I'd ask, *Will this break me or will it refine me?*

Ownership tied it all together. No more blaming teammates, coaches, or circumstances. If we failed, I owned my part. If I wanted change, it started with me.

Take Scott Niedermayer. Here's a guy who could have coasted on talent alone—one of the best defensemen to ever play the game. But every morning at 8 a.m., he was in the gym. Every Anaheim practice, he competed like he was trying to make the team. His standard wasn't about being better than everyone else. It was about being better than he was yesterday.

When you get that? When you get a room full of guys who refuse to negotiate with their standards? That's when special things happen.

THE LESSON FOR LEADERS

People ask me all the time: "How do you build a winning culture?" Like there's some magic formula. Some secret sauce. There isn't. There's just this:

Standards tell us that talent is just our ticket in; sustained success comes from daily choices and consistent self-discipline.

Adversity tells us that every setback (injuries, boos, trades) can become a catalyst for growth and resilience.

Ownership tells us to steer clear of excuses and victimhood, that progress only happens when we take accountability for our performance and decisions.

When I showed up in Anaheim, I could have coasted. New team, prove yourself gradually, feel things out. Instead, I went full throttle from day one. Why? Because that was my standard. And standards aren't situational.

Here's what happened: The young guys—Getzlaf, Perry—they watched everything. How I practiced. How I prepared. How I handled myself after a bad game. They weren't watching because I gave some big speech about standards. They were watching because that's what young players do. They look for players and teammates to emulate. Like I had all those years ago in Hartford.

By living my standards—not preaching them, living them—I gave them permission to elevate their own. I wanted to pay it forward, just like Beast did for me. Getzlaf started showing up earlier. Perry started taking practice battles personally. That's how culture changes. Not through mission statements or team meetings. Through individuals deciding their personal standards are non-negotiable, then living that truth where everyone can see it.

You want to transform your organization? Your team? Your family? Stop trying to change everyone else. Start with your own standards. Make them visible. Make them consistent. Make them non-negotiable.

Watch what happens next.

ONE HELL OF A PARTY

I'd always imagined that winning the Cup would feel like vindication. Like a giant "fuck you" to everyone who'd doubted me. To Hartford for giving up on me. To St. Louis for not building a winner around me. To Edmonton for—well, everything that went down.

But when it happened, I realized something: Success isn't about proving others wrong. It's about proving yourself right.

---

*Success isn't about proving others wrong.
It's about proving yourself right.*

All those years, I'd been fueled by anger. By chips on my shoulder. By wanting to shove success in people's faces. And yeah, that fuel had gotten me pretty far. But it wasn't until I'd started playing for something bigger— for standards, for excellence, for the guys beside me— that I'd actually won.

The Cup wasn't validation that I'd been right all along. It was proof that I'd finally learned to be wrong. Wrong about what mattered. Wrong about what drove excellence. Wrong about what success really meant.

And it was time to celebrate.

June 2007. I was sitting in my backyard in Anaheim, my body feeling like it had been through a car wreck— separated shoulder, bruised ribs, the usual post-playoff inventory. But that didn't matter.

Everybody always asks, "What did you do with your day with the Cup?" Here's how it works: Every player on the winning team gets the Stanley Cup for a day, and I already had my day planned out: July 21. But what I didn't know is that after your team wins the Cup, it stays in the city for a little bit. And if you want to have it, you just . . . ask. (Yep, that was news to me too.)

So of course, I asked. Who wouldn't?

We'd made a plan: At the awards banquet in Toronto—I knew I wasn't going to win anything, just wanted to have some fun—I told my childhood friend Hummer that I had the Cup coming to my house in a couple of days. Hummer is a hell of a cook, and I've always referred to him as my personal chef. So, about a week after we'd won, I hosted a gathering. There were about fourteen people there—my brother and his kids, my parents, Bob Crispin, Hummer. We all sat around and were having some nice wine when the guy delivering the Cup showed up.

"When does the party start?" he asked.

"This is the party," I said. "Do you want to come in and have a glass of wine?"

At first he declined, but when he peeked his head in and saw a low-key dinner with four kids, I guess he thought it was safe to come in. Later that night, after we'd rolled through most of the wine, my brother got a text from a friend—the bassist for the band Sugar Ray, Murphy Karges. He asked if he could get a picture with the Cup, so we told him to come on over. He showed up with producer McG, and then my brother had a brilliant idea.

"Why don't you guys play my brother's Cup Party on the twenty-first?" he asked Murphy as we chilled outside by the fireplace. (As a kid from Dryden, I still can't believe I am typing that sentence.) They reached out to lead singer Mark McGrath to clear the date, then hung up the phone and looked at me.

"If you pay for the roadies to set everything up, we're in."

Next thing I knew, I'd booked Sugar Ray for my Cup Party—and it wasn't just any party. We ended up pouring the band booze out of the Cup in a nightclub I created in my basement. We had a big shaker down there, an epic night people still talk about to this day and one I'll never forget.

After that night, I had time to reflect on the glory of holding the Cup, and it dawned on me: The destination is just geography. The journey is everything. I thought about it all. About standards mattering. About not being able to cheat the process. About the game humbling you.

The destination is just geography.
The journey is everything.

That's the paradox of success: You have to want it desperately enough to do the work, but you can't need it so desperately that the work becomes about the wrong things.

Standards. Process. Character. Team.

Everything else—the trophies, the parades, the vindication—that's just noise.

That's true. It's also true that some noise, like the sounds of Sugar Ray pulsing out of your own nightclub with the Stanley Cup on display, sounds sweeter than the rest.

A couple years later, I heard rumors that Anaheim was shopping me around at the trade deadline to see what my value was. When I wasn't traded, I figured the draft was when the ball was going to drop. I had one year left on my contract, and Anaheim was going in a different direction. In the end, it came down to two teams that were willing to give Anaheim what they wanted: Philadelphia and San Jose.

Yes, San Jose.

I was public enemy number one in that city, which would have been interesting. After all, we'd played them three years in a row in St. Louis in the playoffs (with mixed results) and had formed a deep rivalry. I was always an extremely physical player, and they probably didn't like how I was pushing some of their star players around. I remember when one of their fans came down to the bench and screamed at me. I promptly sprayed them with water. I learned later that when they'd complained, the usher had said something like, "Well, why the hell did you leave your seat and go down there?" If I got shit from the media or the fans in any city, I was always the kind of player and person who was going to give it right back.

Suffice it to say that sports fans have long memories. Plus, I'm pretty sure there was no way Bob Murray and Anaheim were going to trade me to a team in the same division, very likely haunting them every single game. It made more sense to move me to the Eastern Conference, to Philly.

And off I went, on June 26, 2009, to become a Philadelphia Flyer.

By then, I'd learned that trades weren't setbacks—they were checkpoints. Each one tested what I stood for, what I could endure, and what I'd take ownership of when the ice got thin.

I didn't know it yet, but I was nearing the end of the line. The final chapter in a long trade tree.

CHAPTER 6

The Trade Tree

Every trade tells a story. Some are about timing, some about money, some about ego. Together, they form a map of my career—five cities, four trades, nineteen years of learning what loyalty really means in professional sports.

The Trade Tree isn't a résumé—it's a study in how the business works, and what it costs to stay true to your standards when everything around you keeps shifting.

November 11, 2011. Winnipeg, Manitoba. I'm on the ice, and I know—not think, not hope, not wonder—I *know* this is it. My last shift as an NHL player.

The stick feels wrong in my hands. My right eye, the one that took a stick blade less than one month earlier, can't track the puck properly. Everything's blurry on that side, like looking through a windshield in the rain.

My head's pounding—not the usual postgame ache, but something deeper, meaner. The kind of pain that tells you the machine's breaking down for good.

I coast to the bench after the buzzer. Flyers lose, but I'm done.

In the locker room, I sit in my stall longer than usual. Guys are stripping gear, talking about dinner plans, the next game. Normal shit. But I'm cataloging: eighteen years, five teams, 1,167 regular-season games, 173 playoff games. One Stanley Cup. Two more trips to the Finals. And now, at thirty-seven, my body's finally saying what it's been trying to tell me for years: *Enough*.

I pull off my skates for the last time as a player. No ceremony. No announcement. Just me and the equipment guy who's been packing my gear for three years. He knows without asking—you can always tell when a guy's done. There's a look. A way of moving that says the fight's gone out of them.

"Need anything else, Prongs?" he asks.

"Nah. I'm good."

But I wasn't good. I was a thirty-seven-year-old with a scrambled brain, a fucked-up eye, and a résumé that read like a road map of professional sports' ugly truths: You're only as valuable as your last game. Loyalty flows one direction in professional sports, and I was okay with that. And every goodbye is really just business dressed up as personal.

That night started me thinking about all the trades, all the "it's not you, it's us" conversations, all the times I'd been told I was "family" right before they shipped me out like freight. Four trades. Four lessons in how this business really works.

HARTFORD: THE FIRST CUT

Right before I got traded from Hartford, Paul Holmgren came to my hometown of Dryden to check in and see where my head was as well as to do some fishing. Not metaphorically—literally I took him out on a boat, and we talked about the future, how I was going to be the cornerstone of the franchise. We caught Musky and chatted about building a championship team around me.

"You're our guy," he said, reeling in a decent-sized fish. "This is going to be your team in the not-too-distant future."

I was twenty years old. I believed him.

Fast-forward a few days to July 27, 1995. I'd been traded to St. Louis, where the GM was Mike Keenan. A big-time trade—for Brendan Shanahan, a fifty-goal scorer who had become a fan favorite with his physical style and scoring ability.

At least they got value. That's what I told myself, trying to process how "you're our franchise player" became "pack your shit" in the span of less than a few months. Welcome to the NHL, kid. First lesson: Words mean nothing. Contracts mean something. Performance means everything.

Looking back, I'm sure Hartford had been shopping me for weeks, but I don't think Holmgren knew when we were on that fishing trip. That didn't change the fact that it felt like betrayal. But here's what that taught me: If they'll trade a second-overall pick who's shown he can play, they'll trade anybody. Heck, Wayne Gretzky got traded. Nobody's safe. Nobody's special. You're an asset with a depreciation schedule, and the moment your value peaks or you might start to decline, they'll cash you in.

Thirty years later, I can appreciate the lesson. Back then, it just hurt. But hurt's a teacher too, if you're smart enough to listen.

GATEWAY CITY: THE PROVING GROUND

St. Louis in 1995 was where failed prospects went to either resurrect their careers or confirm they were busts. I was almost twenty-one, fresh off being labeled a disappointment in Hartford, walking into a locker room with Brett Hull, Al MacInnis, Grant Fuhr, and a bunch of veterans who'd seen plenty of young guns flame out.

The narrative was already written: "Former second-overall pick couldn't cut it in Hartford, dealt for Brendan Shanahan straight up."

In hockey trades, when you're the young guy going for the established star, you're still a prospect with potential. The lottery ticket. The "maybe he'll figure it out" piece.

Mike Keenan was coaching then. I vividly recall the first day of training camp when we had our physical testing. I failed miserably. Dead last for all the skaters, with one lone exception—Grant Fuhr, our goalie.

Let's just say Keenan . . . well, he was not pleased. Always a direct communicator—something I'd come to appreciate as time went on—he let the world know about it, ripping me both in the media and behind closed doors. Looking back now, I can see the moment for what it was: I still hadn't figured out how to be a true pro. The pressure only seemed to intensify as more eyeballs and expectations were on me before I'd even played one game with the Blues.

I'd be lying through my teeth if I told you those first years in St. Louis felt like a breeze. I was young and very much trying to adjust. A new city, a new team, a new place to fit in. Being traded for a fan favorite and beloved teammate is not easy. I had massive shoes to fill, and I was still trying to figure out who I was both on and off the ice.

On top of that, the Blues fans absolutely did not start neutral, and I can't say I blamed them. They hated me from the outset. I was traded for their beloved star player, and they let me know about it. I didn't help the cause by showing up to training camp in poor shape, and struggling to find my game early only threw fuel on the fire. That's when the intensity of the boobirds picked up. St. Louis had seen enough redemption projects to know most don't work out. At first, I was skating by (literally) on talent, struggling to find my footing.

But eventually, I started living by my standards and taking ownership of my decisions. I "showed up" every night. When you throw your body in front of slap shots, when you fight guys to protect your teammates—they take notice.

As you know from chapter 4, by year three in St Louis, I was nominated for the Norris Trophy. By year five, I'd won it. And the Hart Trophy. MVP of the entire league.

You know what I thought about during my acceptance speech? Hartford trading me. All the people who thought I was a bust at twenty-one. All the people who helped me. All the people who believed in me. I could see how small my circle had gotten over the years, how much smaller it was likely to get before I was done. You find out real quick in this business who your true friends are.

Sometimes rejection is just redirection. Sometimes being unwanted by one team is exactly what you need to become essential to another. But you've got to do the work. You've got to embrace the suck. You've got to prove it every single night.

Nine years in St. Louis. Nine years of bleeding blue. Then they traded me too.

EDMONTON: THE BUSINESS OF LOYALTY

I know some of you have been waiting for this one. Here's the full story.

The night I got traded to Edmonton, August 3, 2005, I'd gone to a friend's thirtieth birthday party and consumed a plethora of alcoholic beverages. I had a good buzz going when I found out about the trade.

There's your vulnerability. There's your truth. Not exactly the story they put on hockey cards.

My phone rang. It was my agent. I ducked into a quiet room, half-drunk, thinking I was headed to Los Angeles, Florida, maybe Boston. Those were the teams we had heard whispers about.

"Edmonton," he said.

Edmonton? Nobody mentioned fucking Edmonton.

On our way home, Lauren and I stopped at a bookstore. She asked the clerk, "Do you have any books about Edmonton?"

The woman looked at her like she'd asked for books about the North Pole. "Why would anyone want to go there?"

Welcome to our new life.

Here's where I fucked up—and where the story you think you know goes sideways. Lauren and I had talked it through that night. We talked about signing my Qualifying Offer with Edmonton—a place Lauren had never even been to yet—and decided to give it a try for one year.

Sign my qualifying offer—one year at $7.2 million—then reevaluate. We'd just lost an entire season to the lockout, and my contract had been rolled back 24 percent. Going from St. Louis to Edmonton for just one year? We could handle that. Then, we could evaluate and see what we wanted to do from there. Then she went to bed

But at 1 a.m., my agent called back. "They want to talk contract. They don't want you playing on a one-year deal. They cannot afford a contract with $7 million in the number."

I should've said no. Should've said I need to sleep on it. Should've said I need to talk to my wife. Instead, sitting in my home office, several more beers deep, we started negotiating.

By 2 a.m., I'd agreed to five years.

Lauren went to bed thinking I would sign for one year. That was the plan. Test it out, see if Edmonton worked for our family, then decide.

"Five years," I told her the next morning.

The silence that followed was louder than any arena crowd.

"You made a five-year commitment about our lives without talking to me? While you were drunk?"

No excuses. That was my standard. So I owned it.

"Yes. I fucked up. I let my agent drive the conversation, I was drinking, and I made a decision that affects our entire family without including you. There's no excuse for that."

But here's where standards really matter—not in avoiding mistakes, but in how you respond to them.

I could've blamed my agent. Could've blamed the alcohol. Could've blamed the injuries. Could've blamed the pressure. Instead, I owned it.

You want to talk about breaking trust? You want to talk about the moment a marriage gets tested? I was telling my wife that I'd just committed five years of her life to a city she'd never lived in, never been to, in a country she wasn't from, with two kids under three, without even asking her opinion.

She was furious—and she had every right to be.

But here's what the rumors got wrong, what the narrative missed: This wasn't about Lauren hating Canada. This wasn't about some of the bullshit rumors that never happened. This was about me making a massive life decision at 2 a.m. without consulting my partner. This was about trust. This was about respect. This was about me fucking up in a way that had nothing to do with hockey and everything to do with being a husband.

I knew it wasn't working by November. Not the team . . . the situation. The promise I'd failed to keep.

As I mentioned earlier in the book, I told my agent: "I'm done after this year. Start figuring out how to make it happen."

From November to June, I played every game knowing I was leaving. Do you understand what that's like? Suiting up every night for fans who love you, teammates who trust you, knowing you're going to break their hearts? But I'd already broken a more important trust. I'd chosen my career over my family once. I wasn't doing it again.

After we lost Game 7 in Carolina on June 17, 2006, the news broke almost immediately. I flew home the next morning and had our rental furniture picked up. Then I left the following day. Rumors spread—can't be that he screwed up. Can't be that he made a bad decision. Must be his American wife.

None of the rumors were accurate. The truth was: I'd made a promise to my wife, broken it, and spent a year trying to make it right.

The Edmonton trade taught me something Hartford hadn't: Sometimes you're the bad guy in somebody else's story. Sometimes you're the one who has to eat the blame. Sometimes protecting what matters means letting people hate you.

I could have stayed an Oiler. Could have played out the contract. Could have kept collecting checks. And destroyed my marriage.

Instead, and I'll say it (and do it) until the day I die: I choose family first.

ANAHEIM: THE REDEMPTION

We won the Cup in Anaheim. You know that story.

But even Anaheim—even after everything, proving I could be the missing piece—lasted just three years. By

2009, the financial crisis had destroyed Southern California. The team wanted to go in a different direction and needed to shed salary. The new GM wanted his own guys and to put his own stamp on this team.

I knew they were trading me. They'd been shopping me at the trade deadline and right up to the draft. But I wanted Bob Murray to admit to my face that they were letting me go. I wanted closure. One night in Vegas prior to the NHL awards at 2 a.m., I met with Bob at a casino table. I was tired. He was tired. But we both knew why we were there.

"I don't want to insult you," he kept saying.

"Just tell me the number."

"Something with a four in it."

At that point, I was making $6.25 million. The cap was going up. Market value said I should get a raise, and this guy wants to pay me $4.5 million after I helped them win the Cup?

"That's not insulting," I said. "That's just stupid."

Ten days later, I was a Flyer.

Thanks for the motivation, Bob.

PHILADELPHIA: THE FINAL TRANSACTION

I'd wanted a four-year deal, one that would have taken me to the ripe old age (in hockey) of forty. A four-year deal, and the market said I was worth $7 million-plus.

I always knew the market set my value, just like I knew the bigger picture was always about winning as a team. If I'd wanted, I could have tried to get eighty points per year and then some, but that would have hurt my defense, which would have hurt our chances of winning . . . you get the picture. I wasn't about to force it every power play just to get "the numbers." I always cared more about my team winning.

Philly agreed with our valuation—they knew what I was worth—but they were not fine with how that number would hit their salary cap. I ended up still getting every dollar of my deal; they just extended the contract to make the annual cap hit smaller. Against the rules? Nope, not at the time. A little, eh . . . strategic? Yep. But look, they weren't the first big-market team to spend money for good players, so back then, it was win-win-win.

To top it off, it was Paul Holmgren. The same guy who'd coached me as a player in Hartford was now GM in Philadelphia, trading for me again.

"Second time's the charm," he said when we finalized the deal.

The symmetry was perfect. Too perfect. Like the universe was setting up one last lesson about how circular this business can be. The guy who taught me some early lessons was bringing me to my last stop.

Philadelphia embraced me immediately. It was a different kind of love than St. Louis. Harder. More demanding. These fans had been waiting for a Cup since their last in 1975, a *long* quarter-century plus. They didn't want potential. They wanted banners.

We gave them a great run in 2009–2010, all the way to the Finals, but lost in six games to Chicago. I played through injuries that should've ended my season. Injured my knee in the second round against Boston and had two M&M-sized chunks of cartilage removed after the playoffs were over. A broken hand the next year, followed by a back surgery, cost me the opportunity to finish the season with my teammates in the playoffs.

You try to tape it up, shoot yourself full of whatever makes the pain stop, and you play. That's what you do. But bodies have limits. Even mine.

On October 24, 2011, I took a stick to the eye from Mikael Grabovski in a game against the Maple Leafs. Eye injury and concussion.

And it wasn't just "any" concussion. Look, I have sustained a number of concussions, and when I first started playing at a higher level, that term didn't really exist. We commonly called a knock to the head "a stinger," "seeing stars," or "getting your bell rung." The eye trauma I sustained made this one a totally different animal. Bright lights bothered me tremendously. I would get nauseous when driving my car. I wore sunglasses at night while driving so the oncoming car lights wouldn't aggravate my eyes or head.

I had always had a sixth sense on the ice that someone was near me or inbound, and I no longer had that feeling.

I used to be able to sense someone coming around the corner as I walked throughout my house. After the stick to the eye, I would routinely get startled by my wife and kids. One time my son Jack came running around the corner in our house and jokingly jumped out to scare me. I was on the verge of throwing punches at him; it completely unglued my senses. There were so many more moments like this.

I felt myself going into a dark place—the headaches, the light sensitivity, the nausea, the fogginess. I had to wear shades at all times—even, as I mentioned, at night, because the headlights would send me spiraling. I couldn't go over a bridge without feeling like I was going to throw up. I still tried to play and push through it, still hit guys and got hit back, feeling like I was going a little bit more crazy with each crushing headache after. Performance wise, even though I felt like I was still one of the top defensemen in the league, I could tell I wasn't myself on the ice.

Finally, after seeing a handful of doctors, we found one who could help attack my vestibular concussion.

Here's what my wife, Lauren, says about the day the eye injury happened and the ways it came to affect our lives:

The phone was ringing off the hook. The Flyers' trainer called me and told me to sit tight while they assessed the situation. They had a hard time even getting a peek at the eye because Chris was in so much pain, and of course the last thing he wanted was a bright light in his injured eye. Once he got to the hospital, the doctors placed drops in his eye and bandaged it with a shield. It was a situation of watchful waiting until the massive blood hematoma in the corner of the right eye dissipated and healed.

With that, we were told that he should get plenty of rest over the next week and then be re-evaluated. There were a lot of pills. Chris lived in our dark bedroom for a solid week. This is the part that I would like to forget forever.

When Chris would get up to use the bathroom, he couldn't keep his balance to walk just ten feet. I would literally have to guide him, carry a lot of his weight, and stand by his side the whole time until I got him back to the bed. He was either going to collapse or vomit. Many times he began to buckle at the knees and we'd just barely make it back to the bed.

In all the years I watched my husband play, he dominated the game! He controlled every play on the ice, calming things down when necessary and escalating things when it was warranted. He always knew where everybody was on the ice, who was on the ice, and who was coming out next onto the ice. He was totally immersed in the games he was playing. Chris was born with this gift—and now it was gone. We all knew it!

Saturday, November 19, vs. the Winnipeg Jets was officially his last NHL game. His symptoms were getting worse, and now even he felt he was in danger of getting hurt. It broke his heart, my heart, our kids' hearts, his parents' hearts, and the Flyer fans' hearts. Chris wasn't able to walk away from the game on his own terms, but it was the right choice.

The funny thing is that after it happened, after going from doctor to doctor to try to figure out what the hell was going on and feeling more out of control than ever, I finally flew to Pittsburgh to see a specialist who had some notoriety from working with professional football and hockey players. I felt comfortable talking to him, and we went through a battery of tests. He poked and prodded and reviewed my whole medical file—all the surgeries, concussions, injuries. I'll never forget when he looked up and said to me, "This is crazy. You mean you are still playing? I can't believe that. You're done, Chris."

I didn't want him to be right, but I knew he was.

The Flyers knew it too. Lauren and I are forever grateful that Ed Snider, the Flyers' longtime owner, allowed us to go home to St. Louis so I could recover and heal even though I had five years left on my contract. A double blessing, as it also allowed Lauren to spend time with her dad, who was very ill. He passed away about a month after we returned to St. Louis, giving them precious time together.

As for me? I wear glasses now, but there is one thing that corrective lenses can't fix: That stick to the eye ended my career.

Another transaction, this time involuntary.

The final trade: from player to civilian.

BETTER, NOT BITTER

People ask if I'm bitter about the trades. Four teams. Four transactions.

My answer? Nope. Not one bit. Wouldn't trade any of it. (No pun intended.)

Because here's what they miss: I'm not the same player without those trades. Maybe I coast in Hartford, never develop that chip on my shoulder. Maybe I get comfortable in St. Louis, stop pushing to improve. Maybe Edmonton doesn't teach me to choose family over career. Maybe Anaheim doesn't show me what wanting to win for the right reasons feels like.

Every trade prepared me for the next challenge. Every rejection built resilience. Every fresh start taught me something I couldn't learn staying comfortable.

You know what's funny? The trades I hated most taught me the most. Hartford's betrayal taught me self-reliance. Edmonton's mess taught me ownership. Even that insulting Anaheim offer taught me to bet on myself . . . again.

The business of hockey can be brutal. Loyalty's a one-way street that only flows toward ownership and fans. But inside that brutality, if you're paying attention, are the best lessons you'll ever learn about resilience, adaptation, and controlling what you can control.

These days, when I speak to business groups, someone always asks about handling organizational change, about being resilient when your company gets acquired or your department gets restructured. I tell them about the Trade Tree. About four fresh starts. About learning to thrive in chaos because chaos is the only constant.

"But how do you not take it personally?" they ask.

Who says I didn't? I took every trade personally. Personally motivated me. Personally drove me. Personally made me better.

The difference is I didn't let it personally paralyze me. Instead, I let it power me.

Your company doesn't owe you loyalty. Your boss doesn't owe you forever. The only person who owes you anything is the one staring at you in the mirror. And what you owe that person is simple: Show up. Work harder than everyone expects. Make yourself too valuable to trade until they trade you anyway. Then do it again somewhere else.

Because in the end, you're not a victim of the Trade Tree. You're not a passenger.

You're the fucking gardener. And every trade is just another chance to grow.

My home in Dryden.

Pronger Family (Chris, four years old)

Dryden TeePees

Dryden Apollos

Kenora AAA (Hostess Cup)

Dryden Eagles (high school, 1989–1990)

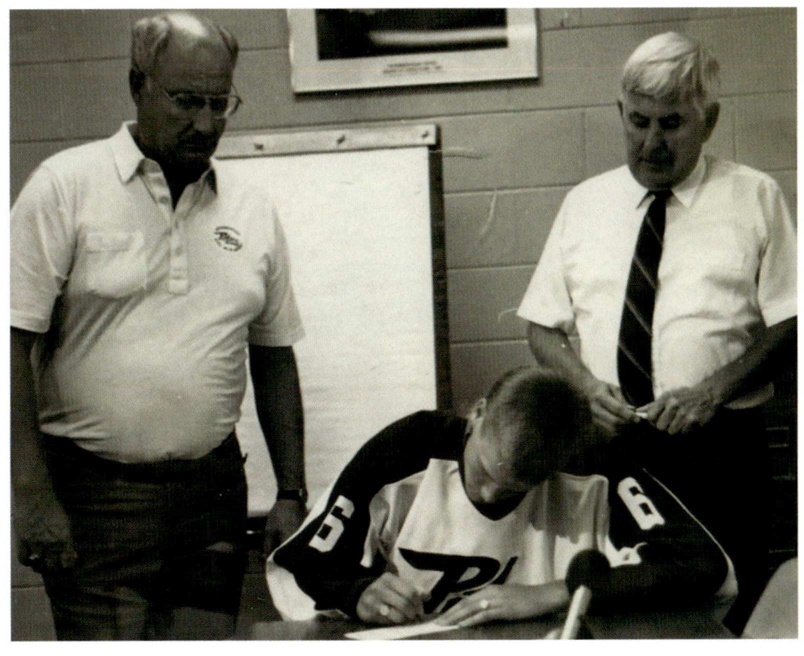

Peterborough Petes signing day (Aug. 1991)

Peterborough Petes (draft year 1992–1993)

NHL Draft top prospects (June 1993)

Chatting with "THE" Gordie Howe at the Hartford Whalers draft table.

Warmup with D partner and mentor Brad McCrimmon aka "Beast."

Baby face, my first year in St. Louis (third year pro).

Nagano Olympics (Feb. 1998)

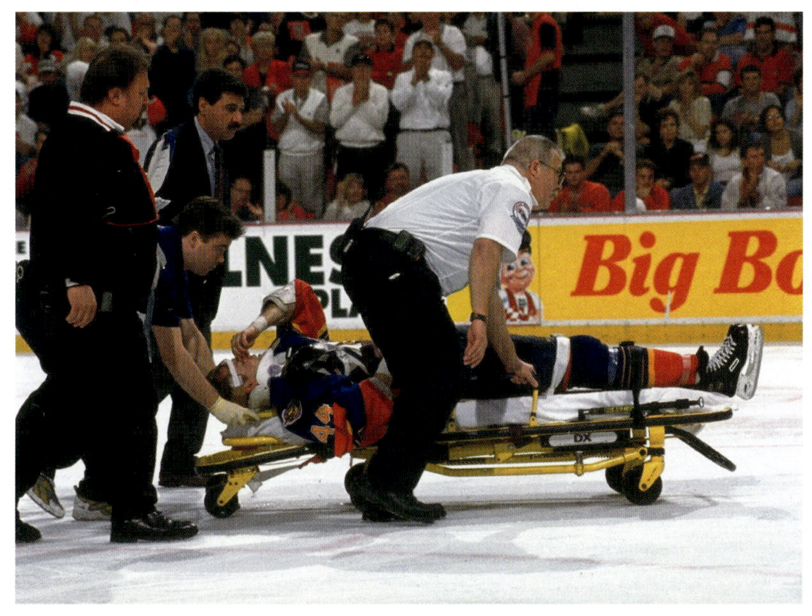

Stretchered off the ice in Joe Louis Arena (1998 commotio cordis).

Youngest captain in St. Louis Blues history just shy of my twenty-third birthday.

Norris Trophy and Hart Trophy winner (1999–2000 season)

Lauren pregnant with our first child (Jack) and my ACL surgery and wrist reconstruction.

Teemu Selänne hit from 2002 Olympics in Salt Lake City.

2002 Olympic gold medal winning team Canada.

One of the many payback opportunities on Teemu Selänne.

First taste of the Stanley Cup Finals with the Edmonton Oilers.

*Still the only player in NHL history to score a penalty shot goal
in a Stanley Cup Final (SCF) game.*

Slap shot

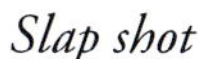

Practice makes perfect!

Best feeling ever. Thirteen years in the making.

Rivals, turned teammates, turned CHAMPIONS! The hand-off we dreamed of.

My brother Sean helped me lift the Stanley Cup. Family dream fulfilled!

Family photo taking in the Stanley Cup scene.

2007 Stanley Cup Champions . . . never gets old saying that.

Mark McGrath of Sugar Ray enjoying a taste from the Stanley Cup.

Former high school coach Jack McMaster soaking up some Cup time.

Old high school D partners celebrate.

Chris Hancock and I (1989–1990)

My boys, Jack (6) and George (4), hanging with me at the 2008 All-Star Game in Atlanta.

My grandpa (Erki) helping me hold my 1000th game stick.

Giroux and Briere showing some excitement after a SCF goal.

Sometimes you have to negotiate a little with the officials.

Induction into the Triple Gold Club (Fetisov & Larionov pictured).

Second Olympic gold medal in Vancouver (2010).

Olympic gold medal winning team Canada (2010).

Honored to be the 18th Captain of the Philadelphia Flyers.

On the ice in pain after being struck in the eye from a stick.

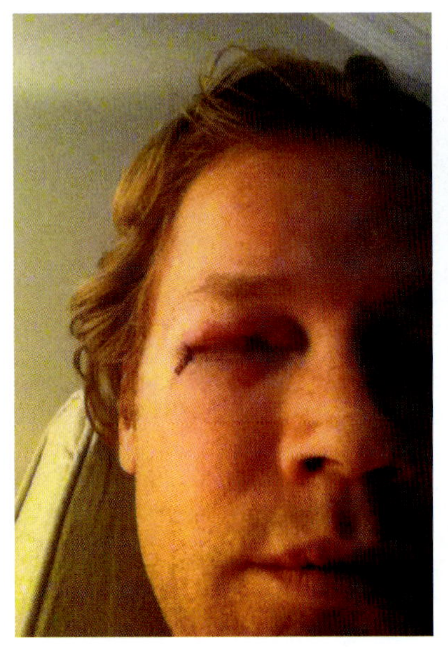

Carnage following a stick to the eye against Toronto.

Short lived return with a visor (five games played).

Eye rehab looks weird, doesn't it?

2015 Hockey Hall of Fame induction ceremony.

Hockey Hall of Fame plaque.

#44 retired in St. Louis on January 16, 2022.

2017 NHL Top 100 Announcement in LA.

It is a privilege.

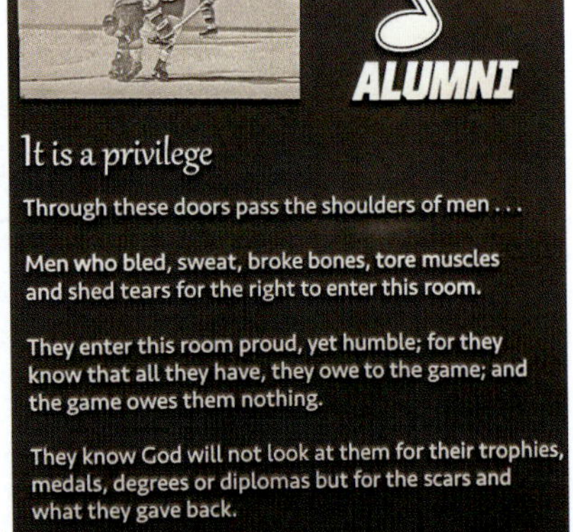

Broadcasting for a St. Louis Blues game.

Keynote speech on team building.

Love being in front of a big crowd.

My heart! Family picture (2025).

ACT III

Standards + Adversity + Ownership = Success

CHAPTER 7

Finding Clarity
Beyond the Ice

On October 1, 2023, I quit drinking.

No dramatic story. No rock bottom with flashing lights. Just a decision that had been building for years, accelerated by seeing myself through my kids' eyes. They weren't angry. They were disappointed. That hit different.

"I'm done drinking," I told Lauren.

She nodded. This time, we both knew I meant it.

The clarity that followed wasn't immediate. It came in waves, each one revealing something I'd been too foggy to see before.

But to understand where that clarity led, you need to understand where the fog began.

THE DRIFT

December 11, 2011, was my last NHL game, the one against Winnipeg. One day you're Chris Pronger, NHL defenseman, veteran, all-star, former MVP—every minute scheduled, every day structured. The next day you're Chris Pronger . . . what?

Think about it. For eighteen years, my life had been dictated by the schedule. September meant training camp. October through April meant eighty-two games plus playoffs. Summer meant structured training. Every day had a purpose, a place to be, a role to fill. Team meeting at 10. Practice at 11. Meal at 1. Nap at 3. Pre-game at 5. Game at 7. Postgame interviews, bus, flight. Repeat, repeat, repeat.

Then it stops. Just . . . stops.

That first year was supposed to be about healing. My eye was damaged from the stick. The concussion symptoms lingered—light sensitivity, headaches, the works. I'd sit in dark rooms, trying to let my brain heal, trying to figure out what came next.

My eyes seem to get tired so much faster these days, so I always have my sunglasses with me. I have also doubled down on the importance of eating properly and taking care of my body. After sixteen surgeries, I need to make sure I continue to lift and stay as strong as possible. Lauren and I are firm believers in nourishing the mind, body, and soul with holistic healing therapies. I have learned so much from her and how to continue on the path of recovery through implementing very simple therapies and clean eating. I am still a little light-sensitive and loud noises bother me, but overall these issues are all manageable. I am grateful to be able to live a full life.

There will always be effects of the concussion, but I now know ways to avoid triggers. I manage my head issues by making sure I don't overexert myself, yet continue to push myself in that regard so that I keep pushing my limits. I will forever be grateful to the ones that got me to the place I am today: my wife, children, trainers, doctors, and many more.

But that healing took time to get to. And the truth is that somewhere between rehabilitation and reality, I found myself filling the void hockey left with something else. Business lunches were my new game days. And alcohol? That became the thread connecting it all.

The structure that had defined eighteen years? Gone. The standards that had taken me from Hartford's boos in 1993 to the Hall of Fame in 2015? Still there, technically. But standards without purpose are like a Ferrari without a destination—impressive but ultimately pointless.

You know what they don't tell you about retirement? It's not the money you miss. It's not even the game. It's knowing exactly who you are and what you're supposed to do when you wake up.

For eighteen years, I was Chris Pronger, number 44, defenseman. Clear role. Clear purpose. Clear identity.

Now? I was just another retired athlete trying to figure out Act Two. I thought I had prepared for the end, but it didn't take long for me to realize I wasn't ready at all for the twists and turns that awaited.

BUILDING WITHOUT A BLUEPRINT

The businesses started organically, the way most good things do—by accident and necessity.

Lauren and I co-founded Well Inspired Travels, a boutique luxury travel company. When friends started asking for recommendations, then referrals, then full planning, we saw an opportunity. Not just a business, but a way to share what we'd learned. High-end, tailor-made travel experiences for elite athletes, entertainers, CEOs, and business owners—people who, like us, had unique pressures and specific needs.

My brother, Sean, and I also launched a Canadian whisky brand in 2022. Two Pronger boys who'd grown up in Dryden, Ontario, where winter lasted eight months and warmth came in bottles. The irony wasn't lost on me—building a booze business while trying to figure out my own relationship with the product.

Then there were the investments. Real estate deals. Stock portfolios. Angel investments in startups. This is where the standards framework really started to evolve— but that wisdom came at a price. In fact, the chaos of all those trades, combined with the market crash of 2008, taught me expensive lessons. To this day, I am ever-evolving and gaining new understanding and perspective. If a deal goes south, I don't fall into victimhood. I take a harder look at it: What went wrong? Why didn't it work? How can I own what happened, stay in line with my standards, and use this adversity as a stepping stone?

Look, let's get real: Any businessperson or investor who tells you they've never lost money is lying. But in a way, it's just like it is on the ice: Growth happens through the failures, through the shots you miss or don't take. Sometimes you win, sometimes you learn. Here's what I discovered along the way: The success pyramid that had saved my hockey career translated perfectly to business. You just had to adjust the inputs.

Sometimes you win, sometimes you learn.

Let me break it down using three key principles that can make or break any deal, project, or goal:

Foundation (Hard Work): Off the ice, the foundational work of the business world is due diligence and intentionality. I always sleep on decisions if I can—a lesson I learned the hard way after the Edmonton debacle—and resist artificial urgency. Why? Because pressured decisions rarely lead to good outcomes. I also pay close attention to the *who*. Who are the players involved in the investment you're looking at? What's at stake, for you and for them? Understanding the full scope of the team you're about to align yourself with is key.

Fuel (Resources): In this case, fuel isn't the stuff of muscles and macros . . . it's money. What is your money going to do for this venture, this business, this investment? How can you optimize that input for maximum output?

Peak (Mindset): Mindset continues to be a difference maker: In the business world, how can you continue to improve upon the investment thesis or business model you currently have? What are you learning from each decision and on each deal to get better?

That might sound simple. It *is* simple. But simple doesn't mean easy.

STANDARDS + ADVERSITY + OWNERSHIP = SUCCESS

Along the way, I also developed a professional speaking platform, drawing on my experiences in sports and business. The turning point came when I stopped trying to be what I thought people wanted—a polished motivational speaker—and started being Chris Pronger, the guy who'd been booed at home by nineteen thousand fans and lived to tell about it.

The message was the one you have already read about throughout this book, the one that began with a simple question in a sports psychologist's office when I was stuck early in my career. His question—*What are your standards?*—spurred me to develop a structure that would guide my hockey career and continues to keep me on track today: Standards + Adversity + Ownership = Success.

Whether I was talking to executives or entrepreneurs, the framework translated. They didn't need another hockey metaphor. They needed someone who'd failed publicly, rebuilt systematically, and could show them how.

I was able to share what I learned in my real estate mistakes that shaped my dealings with people. Now I handle my business this way: character first, deal or opportunity second—which might seem backwards to some. Only if the character is there do I move on to assessing capital, team, concept, etc. In short, today, every deal starts with one question: Are they good people?

With standards, my wins began compounding. But here's what I noticed: The more I succeeded in business, the more I spoke about standards and excellence, the wider the gap grew between what I preached and how I lived. The concussion symptoms made everything far more pronounced, far worse.

What do you get when you take that—being at the mercy of sensitivity to light and sound, losing your peripheral vision, trying to get your mind to catch up to how quick it used to be—and add it to the fear and isolation of COVID as the year 2020 unfolded? For me, a recipe for drinking a whole lot more, as in almost every day. It began to affect me in different ways. With my body getting older and still battling concussion symptoms, I could feel the alcohol as soon as it touched my tongue. After a couple of drinks, I couldn't remember shit—something that had never happened to me before, not even close.

Outwardly, things were going well. But in my house and in my head, things were getting worse, not better. We'd built Well Inspired Travels into a successful boutique firm, but how many family trips had I spent too long being buzzed? I'd launched a whisky brand while becoming too familiar with the product.

The compound effect works both ways. Yes, 1 percent daily improvement leads to being thirty-seven times better in a year. But 1 percent daily deterioration? That compounds too. And it's harder to see because the decline is gradual, acceptable, excusable.

Which brings us back to that big decision to quit.

My kids had been the catalyst. Not through confrontation but through observation. When your adult children start being embarrassed at family gatherings or other events because they don't want to see you "in party mode" again, when they stop bringing friends around because they're not sure which version of dad they'll get, when their disappointment becomes palpable—that's your wake-up call.

Or it should be.

For me, it was. The same clarity that had come in Dr. Miller's office in 1996 returned. Different problem, same solution: standards.

What were my standards around alcohol? I didn't have any. I had preferences, habits, patterns. But standards? Non-negotiable daily behaviors regardless of how I felt? None.

So I created one: zero alcohol.

Not "drink responsibly." Not "only on weekends." Not "just wine with dinner."

Zero.

Because here's what thirty years of standards taught me: Gray areas are where standards go to die. "Just one" becomes "just tonight" becomes "just this week" becomes "just like always."

Here's what thirty years of standards taught me: Gray areas are where standards go to die.

STANDARDS 2.0

The clarity that followed wasn't just about seeing clearly—it was about being seen clearly. By my family. By my audiences. By myself.

The same standards that had saved my hockey career now shaped my entire life:

- Working out in the early morning (because champions don't retire from discipline)
- Being present for my family (not just physically—mentally, emotionally, fully)
- Building businesses with purpose (profit matters, but impact matters more)
- Teaching what I learned the hard way (through speaking, writing, mentoring)
- Drinking zero alcohol (non-negotiable, no exceptions, no excuses)

But these aren't just my standards. They're examples. Your standards will be different. Should be different. Must be different. Your adversity will be different and your ownership will be up to you.

Because the gap between who you are and who you could be? That's personal. Individual. Unique as your fingerprint. But the process to close it? That's universal.

You can't give what you don't have. You can't teach what you don't live. You can't raise others' standards while lowering your own.

You can't give what you don't have. You can't teach what you don't live. You can't raise others' standards while lowering your own.

That speaking platform I built is more powerful now because the message and the messenger are aligned. Those businesses I'm growing are clearer because I'm clearer. The investments I'm making are stronger because I'm making those decisions with a clear head and consistent framework.

When people ask why I quit drinking, the answer is simple: I finally applied my own framework to my biggest opponent: myself.

BRIDGING THE GAP

The *adversity* was seeing myself through my family's eyes. The *ownership* was accepting that I'd created this gap between who I was and who I wanted to be. The *standards* became the bridge to close that gap.

In hockey. In business. In life. In clarity.

What about you? What role do adversity, ownership, and standards play in your life, your relationships, your business? Maybe a lot, but maybe a little or not at all. Either way, I believe your clarity moment is coming. Or maybe it's here, reading this, recognizing your own gap between preaching and practicing, between potential and performance, between who you are and who you could be.

The question isn't whether you'll recognize it.

The question is: What will you do when you do?

Because here's the final truth: The same frameworks that can transform your career can transform your life, but only if you have the courage to apply them to yourself first.

What are *your* standards?

Not your goals. Not your dreams. Not what you tell others.

What are your actual, daily, non-negotiable behaviors?

Answer that honestly, and everything else follows.

Or don't, and nothing changes.

Your choice. It always has been.

CHAPTER 8

The Difference Maker's Code

Success is an iceberg, and a lot of people only want to talk about the top that's sticking out of the water.

The winning, the Stanley Cup, the Hart, the Norris, the Olympic golds, the NHL Top 100 Player.

But underneath the surface? There's the real stuff: sacrifices, failures, mistakes. The first-ever successful Darrach Procedure in a professional athlete. Three hand surgeries, ACL surgery, back surgery, a broken jaw, eight suspensions, four trades, a stopped heart, uprooting family, media scrutiny and questions, fan scrutiny and questions, being booed—you name it.

I always knew what I was doing it for, and it wasn't to get to the Hockey Hall of Fame or the rest of the iceberg sticking out of the water.

I did it to be a champion, to win. To be better than I was yesterday. Living by my standards meant remembering that not improving every day meant going backwards.

I know what you're thinking. Sounds like motivational-poster bullshit, right?

Wrong.

Your competition is improving. Right now, while you're reading this, someone who is gunning for your job, your position, your life is getting better. If you're standing still, you're not maintaining—you're falling behind.

When I was playing, this wasn't philosophy. It was survival. Every day I didn't improve, some hungry kid in the minors got one day closer to taking my job.

In business? Same game, different arena. That competitor who looks just "good enough" in your eyes? They're studying your weaknesses. That employee who seems satisfied at a glance? They're updating their LinkedIn profile, networking with C-suite leaders, earning a new certification.

Every day is an opportunity to get better. Not dramatically better. Not transformationally better. Just better. One percent. That's it.

But here's the math that changes everything: One percent better every day compounds to 3,700 percent improvement in a year. Not 37 percent—3,700 percent.

The catch is that you won't see it for months. The results hide like your iceberg getting stronger from underneath, growing sturdier under water. Most people quit during the invisible phase, but champions trust the process.

YOUR BIGGEST ENEMY HAS YOUR ADDRESS

Want to know the biggest obstacle preventing people from success?

Look in the mirror.

It's the victimhood mentality. That voice in your head that says:

- "It's not my fault."
- "If only I had their advantages."
- "The system is rigged."
- "That guy got lucky."

I was right there with you. Twenty-one years old, making more money than my parents ever dreamed of, and I was the victim. Poor me, getting booed. Poor me, pressure's too much. Poor me, nobody understands.

Bullshit. All of it.

The biggest obstacle for people is their mindset. We want to blame others for our lot in life. For what we don't have. For where we're stuck.

But standards don't care about your excuses. They only care about your execution. And they self-destruct when adversity strikes without ownership. I learned that in Hartford, in Edmonton, and even at home when I made the decision about Edmonton. Ownership is what turns standards into action.

---

*Ownership is what turns
standards into action.*

And execution, by the way, might take some time. Are you willing to grind for the life you really want? There isn't a magic pill, a quick fix. Instead, you have to be both patient and proactive. Prepare yourself so that when your chance comes up—or when the opportunity you created through hard work comes to fruition— you can jump on it. Who knows? It might be the lone opportunity you get, and if you haven't put in the work, it'll slip.

The "bare minimum" isn't going to get you any- where. In fact, I've seen a lot of people who think the bare minimum is the work, but the work is actually just the beginning, the baseline. These lessons do not just apply in sports . . . not by a long shot. When I speak with corporate clients and audiences about teamwork, the concepts clearly overlap.

Say you've got a sales quota to sell five hundred units. In the first week, if you hit your numbers, do you go on a holiday? Do you slack off? Maybe you think, *I did my job. That's good enough.*

Hell no, you don't. And why not? Because you know one good week, one solid month, one quota met is not "good enough." It's only a beginning, a milestone on the road toward greatness. Just like there is no "good enough" on championship teams, there is no "good enough" in winning cultures.

If you're smart, when you taste a little bit of success you look around at the rest of your sales team and ask, "Okay, how can I help support you? How can we win as a team here?" The trick to success isn't really that tricky: Have a team-first, company-first, growth-first mindset, and surround yourself with people who do the same.

This isn't lip service. Trust me, it pays off in spades. Because when you do it and you see the rewards, when you get that taste of success, you'll realize that all that iceberg underneath the water has gotten you to this point, that it was all worth it. And I don't know one person who has "won" in sports, business, or life and said, "That was nice, but it was too hard."

What do they say instead?

"Damn. I want that again."

And that's exactly the point of standards.

HOW TO BUILD YOUR CODE (STARTING TODAY)

You want to identify your success code? Here's how: Build your standards, expect adversity, and decide in advance how you'll own your response when you slip.

Start with standards. They're the foundation.

First, figure out where you're going. Not where you hope to go. Where you're *going*.

I wanted to be the best hockey player I could possibly be. Not the kid with potential. Not the washout. The kid who maximized every ounce of talent God gave him.

What does that look like in your world? I would suggest that you do a thorough self-analysis. Start by reflecting on several big questions:

- Who are you?
- Where do you want to go?
- What do you want to be?

Then reverse engineer it. What standards would the person you want to be have? What would they do daily? What would they never do?

That's your blueprint.

THE RESET PROTOCOL

Here's something nobody admits: We all get off track. Me included.

I haven't always followed my pyramid. Had cheat meals that turned into cheat weeks. Missed workouts because I was "too busy." Let the mental game slip because I was comfortable.

The difference between champions and everyone else isn't perfection. It's the speed of the reset. You have one cheat meal, and it turns into another, then another. You're traveling, and workouts get missed. Life gets in the way. Fine. It happens.

But champions recognize it fast and reset faster. Resets are how you practice winning through adversity. The moment you stumble, ownership means you reset without excuses.

No drama. No guilt. No "I'll start Monday." Just reset. Now.

It's actually a good thing when you realize you need a reset. It means your standards are still alive, still talking to you. The dangerous time is when you don't even notice you're off track.

In fact, in moments of difficulty, moments of crisis, moments when you feel like you want to quit, you have to realize something: This is the moment. This is why you trained. Why you leveled up. Why you built that stronger mindset.

It's not for the easy times. Any idiot can succeed when the wind's at their back. It's for the hard times. And if you can stick to your standards for thirty, sixty, ninety days . . . pretty soon that snowball is going to start rolling down the hill, getting bigger and stronger the farther it goes.

That's how standards work: the compound effect. That's how difference makers are built.

If you get stuck along the way, don't ever forget the value of mentors. (P.S. This is true even if you don't get stuck. You'll never know it all.) If you need support or want to learn ways to get better—at your job, at your relationships, at your life—be brave enough to find someone you can learn from and always respect the time they give to you. On the other hand, if you're in a position to mentor or support someone else in something you're great at, take that time. It makes you better. For example, if a member of the media today wants to ask a question about the game, they call me because they know I've got the answer or will get it for them and I'm passionate about this sport. In my case, if someone wants to learn about hockey, I've got all the time in the world.

What do you have all the time in the world to teach? What do you need to work on that might require a mentor or some coaching?

Anybody who tells you they've got it all figured out is lying. Living Standards are about being able to see both sides—where you can make an impact and where you need to improve—at the same time.

THE BINARY CHOICE

Look, if it was easy, everybody could do it.

It's not supposed to be easy . . . which is precisely what makes it worth doing. That's what separates the difference makers from everyone else. We don't run *from* hard. We run *toward* it. Because we know that on the other side of hard is everything we've ever wanted.

*On the other side of hard is
everything we've ever wanted.*

So I'll ask you the same question that Dr. Miller asked me in his tiny office all those years ago. The question that started everything. The question that separates those who dream from those who do: What are your standards? What are the bedrock principles that you live by, whether times are easy or challenging? It might be helpful to break them down into different categories . . .

Personal Standards: What will you demand from yourself when nobody's watching?

Team Standards: What culture are you creating? What behaviors are non-negotiable?

Performance Standards: The natural results of living your personal and team standards.

The difference between good and great isn't talent. I've seen plenty of talented failures. It's not opportunity. I've watched people waste golden chances.

It's standards. It's the code you live by: **Standards. Adversity. Ownership.** That's the Difference Maker's Code. This code is what holds you up when adversity comes—and it will. Will you embrace it or run from it? And when excuses whisper in your ear, will you blame others or take ownership?

Standards. Adversity. Ownership.

Success starts and ends with your standards. Standards aren't what you hope for. They're what you hold yourself to. Every single day. When you're tired. When you're stressed. When nobody's watching.

Especially when nobody's watching.

CONCLUSION
Your Standards, Your Success

January 17, 2022. Enterprise Center, St. Louis. That's the day they retired my jersey, number 44, in all its glory. I remember stepping up to the mic, hearing the applause from the crowd—many of whom were wearing number 44 in celebration. I was—and still am—so proud to be up there with Blues fan favorites and former teammates Brett Hull (#16), Al MacInnis (#2), and many others.

What a moment. And underneath it all, I knew that some of those folks in the bleachers were the same boobirds who had turned on me all those years ago when I was finding my footing after being traded for Shanny. I didn't hold back, sharing the moment with the crowd.

When I said, "I grew up in front of your eyes" to that crowd of Blues fans, I meant it. When I said, "Being booed by you and being cheered by you was instrumental in getting me through adversity and helping me flourish," I meant it. When I said, "I'm extremely honored and humbled to be up there with all these Blues greats," I meant that too.

It was fitting to have my jersey retired in St. Louis—where I met my wife, where my career took its turn, where my legacy stopped becoming an idea and started becoming something I was reaching toward, where I discovered the power of standards.

It goes deeper. Without Hartford, there're no standards. Without Peterborough, no standards. Without standards, there's no Stanley Cup. Without the Cup, there's no Hall of Fame. Without any of it, I'm not writing this book, and you're not reading it.

My point? Every single thing I became started with discovering what I wasn't.

Which means that wherever you're starting from as you're reading this is the right place to be.

From here, we go up.

THE SUCCESS EQUATION

Let's recap what thirty years of getting my ass kicked taught me:

Standards + Adversity + Ownership = Success

That's it. That's the whole formula. Not complicated. Not requiring special talent. Not dependent on where you started or what advantages you had. Just those three elements, applied consistently, no matter what.

Let me prove it:

- Standards without adversity? That's just theory. Untested bullshit.
- Adversity without standards? That's just suffering. Victimhood mentality.
- Standards and adversity without ownership? That's excuses. "If only . . ." thinking.

But when you combine all three? When you set non-negotiable standards, embrace the inevitable adversity, and own every outcome? That's when transformation happens. Not *might* happen. Not *could* happen. *Will* happen.

I've seen it work. In hockey, when I went from feeling the hatred of the boobirds in Hartford and St. Louis to celebrating as a Norris and Hart Trophy winner in St. Louis. In business, building companies after retirement. In my personal life, getting sober at forty-eight and finding clarity I never knew existed. The equation works because it mirrors how life actually operates, not how we wish it would.

MEETING YOU WHERE YOU ARE

Look, I don't know where you are in life as you're reading this. Maybe you're successful but stuck, wondering if this is all there is. Maybe you're in your Hartford moment right now—failing publicly, questioning everything. Maybe you're young, trying to figure out which path to take. Maybe you're starting over at forty or fifty or sixty, thinking it's too late.

No matter what your current circumstances might be, here's what I know: Wherever you are, it's the perfect place to start.

---

*Wherever you are, it's the
perfect place to start.*

Think I had advantages? Let me remind you: I was a twenty-one-year-old making millions who was struggling to play hockey at the NHL level. I had talent—so what? Talent without standards is just wasted potential. I had opportunity—who cares? Opportunity without preparation is just dressed-up failure. I had support—big deal. Support without personal accountability is just enabled mediocrity.

Your situation might be different, but the solution isn't. The same standards that transformed a booed hockey player work for:

- The executive who's plateaued
- The entrepreneur who's struggling
- The parent who's overwhelmed
- The athlete who's injured
- Anyone else who's human

Because standards don't care about your circumstances. They only care about your commitment.

THE THREE QUESTIONS THAT MATTER

When I started working with that sports psychologist in St. Louis, he made me answer three questions. Took me months to answer them honestly. I'm going to save you the time:

1. **What game are you really playing?** Not the surface game. Not the job title or the role you fill. The real game. For me, hockey was never just about hockey. It was about proving I belonged, about becoming someone who couldn't be dismissed. What's your real game?

2. **What does winning look like?** Specific. Measurable. Undeniable. Not "being successful" or "making money" or any of that vague bullshit. For me, winning meant championships, gold medals for Team Canada. It meant hoisting the Stanley Cup. Being inducted into the Hockey Hall of Fame was an added bonus for all the

blood, sweat, and tears in search of excellence! What's your equivalent?

3. **What are you willing to sacrifice?** Because there will be sacrifice. Guaranteed. I gave up the easy path in high school. Changed my habits and learned how to be consistent in St Louis. Gave up comfort every single day for thirty years. Gave up drinking at forty-eight. What will you give up to become who you're capable of being?

Answer those honestly, and you're already ahead of 95 percent of people.

STANDARDS IN ACTION: YOUR 30-DAY CHALLENGE

Enough theory. Enough inspiration. Enough of my story. Time for yours.

Here's your challenge, starting tomorrow morning:

WEEKS 1–2: FOUNDATION

- Pick three standards.* Just three. Make them specific, daily, and measurable.
- Write them down. Put them where you'll see them.
- Track them. Every. Single. Day.
- When you fail (you will), own it and restart. No shame, no beating yourself up. Just reset.

WEEKS 3–4: PRESSURE

- Life will test your standards. Guaranteed. Be ready to withstand it.
- When adversity happens, good. That's what you need. Grow stronger through it.
- Don't modify the standards. Modify your approach.
- Find one person to hold you accountable. Tell them your standards.

DAY 30: ASSESSMENT

- What changed? Not just externally—internally.
- Which standard was hardest to keep? That's your biggest growth area.
- What adversity appeared? That's your teacher. How did you handle it?
- How do you feel? Different, right?

That's one month. Imagine a year. Imagine a decade. Imagine a lifetime of living by standards instead of circumstances.

*If you need help identifying your standards, try pulling from this list or looking to it for inspiration. Something may interest you, or something might click in your brain to help you create something fresh.

PRONGER'S FIFTEEN STANDARDS FOR A PRO MINDSET

- Take Ownership—Take full responsibility for results, good or bad. No excuses, no blame.
- Never Enter the Room Cold—Never walk into a locker room, meeting, or conversation without doing the work first.
- Do What You Say You're Going to Do—Follow through, whether you want to or not. Keep your commitments. Simple as that.
- Start the Day Off Right—Start strong and set the tone before the world can distract you.
- Show Up—Success is built in the small, repeatable actions you refuse to skip.
- Raise Your Bar—Set a baseline for effort and performance that others would call their best.
- Protect Your Bench—Surround yourself only with people who elevate your standards, not lower them.
- Run *Toward* Adversity—Choose the hard path. Pressure creates growth; comfort kills it.
- Get Your Head Right—No complaining, no victimhood. Reframe every obstacle as an opportunity.
- Take Care of Your Health—Energy is a competitive advantage. Treat your body like your greatest asset.

- Eliminate Distractions—Cut out what doesn't move you forward. Guard your time and attention.
- Lead With Discipline, Not Motivation—Motivation fades. Discipline keeps the promise you made to yourself.
- Demand Feedback—Seek it out, learn from it, and adjust without ego.
- Finish What You Start—Half-done work is wasted potential. Follow through until it's complete.
- Play to Win, Not to Participate—Set goals that demand excellence, not just effort.

BONUS

For a downloadable and printable list of standards focused on ownership, discipline, and drive, please visit ChrisPronger.com/standards or scan this QR code:

THE RIPPLE EFFECT

Here's something I didn't understand at twenty-one: When you transform yourself through standards, you transform others by proximity. Your discipline inspires discipline. Your ownership encourages ownership. Your resilience builds resilience.

I see it with my kids now. They see me hit the gym when I don't feel like it. They hear me own my mistakes without excuses. Think they're learning more from my words or my actions?

You influence five people directly. Those five influence five more. Before you know it, your personal standards are creating cultural change. In your family. In your workplace. In your community.

But it starts with you. It starts with a decision. It starts with Standards.

P.S. Thirty years ago, I thought those Hartford and St. Louis fans were my enemies. Turns out they were my teachers. I just wasn't ready for the lesson. Whoever or whatever is booing you right now? That's not your enemy either. That's your opportunity. The question is: Are you ready for it?

EPILOGUE
Letter to My Younger Self

Dear Nineteen-Year-Old Chris,

I'm writing this from a place you can't imagine yet. Not just geographically—though, yeah, you'll end up in some unexpected cities—but from a completely different life. Right now, you're sitting in your apartment at 2 a.m., replaying tonight's game in your mind where you went minus-three. Again. The boos are still ringing in your ears. You're wondering if everyone's right about you being a bust.

First, let me tell you something that'll sound like bullshit but isn't: Those fans booing you? They're giving you a gift. You just won't unwrap it for about five years.

I know what you're going through. The weight of that $7 million contract feels like an anchor around your neck. You can't sleep. You're drinking too much. The pressure's so intense you actually hope to be a healthy scratch just so you don't have to fail in public again.

Here's what's really happening: You're learning what doesn't work. And kid, that's just as valuable as learning what does. Maybe more.

THE FAILURES THAT SAVE YOU

That minus-five game against Boston coming up? The one where you can't even look at Dad afterward? That's going to teach you that talent without preparation is just potential energy going nowhere. The trade to St. Louis that'll blindside you? That's going to show you nobody owes you anything, no matter what promises they make. That fuckup with the Edmonton contract? That's going to teach you *every* decision is worth sleeping on. And that it's always wise to include the people you love most when weighing big choices like that. (Oh, yes, you'll have a special someone; I'll tell you more about her a little later.)

That playoff run in Edmonton where you'll lose Game 7 of the Stanley Cup Finals? That one's going to hurt. You'll lie in a Colorado house with your knee locked up and your elbow looking like a grapefruit, wondering if it's all worth it. But that loss is going to show you the difference between good and great, between almost and enough.

Even that career-ending eye injury in Philly—yeah, your career does end, but not for another eighteen years, so relax—that's going to force you to discover who Chris Pronger is without hockey. Spoiler alert: You figure it out.

LISTEN TO BEAST (EVENTUALLY YOU WILL)

Brad McCrimmon is about to walk into your life. The Whalers organization is bringing him in specifically to mentor you. You're going to be a complete numbskull to him. "Yeah, sure Beast" is going to become your catchphrase, and not in a good way.

He's going to tell you about preparation. About standards. About how being a professional means more than just showing up. You're not going to listen. You're nineteen and making more money than him and think that means you know better.

You don't.

But here's the thing—Brad's going to be patient with you. He's going to keep teaching even when you're not learning. And one day, about fifteen years from now, he's going to hand you a letter for your thousandth game. Then, you'll finally understand everything he tried to tell you. He's going to laugh and say, "Remember when you didn't listen to one damn word?" And you'll both know how much was saved by his patience and lost by your pride.

It's okay. Mentors understand that sometimes wisdom needs time to ferment.

YOUR BODY'S GOING TO TAKE A BEATING

Let me prepare you for something: The bill comes due. Every hit you take, every fight you don't avoid, every time you play through injury because that's what warriors do—it all gets tallied up.

You're going to separate your shoulder and keep playing. You're going to have floating bone chips in your knee and keep playing. You're going to take a puck to the chest that literally stops your heart, and after it restarts, you're going to want to keep playing.

By the end, you'll have had five knee surgeries, three hand and wrist surgeries, a back surgery, multiple concussions, and vision problems that end your career. You'll wake up some mornings at fifty feeling every single one of those 1,167-plus games.

Worth it? Every single second. Because those scars are going to be your credentials when you teach others about sacrifice and standards. But take care of your body better than I did. The glory fades; the pain doesn't.

ABOUT THAT DRINKING

You're using alcohol to handle the pressure right now. I get it. When you're getting booed by your home fans and everything feels like it's falling apart, that bottle seems like the only friend who doesn't judge.

Here's something I wish I'd figured out at twenty-one instead of forty-eight: The bottle's not your friend. It's a thief. It steals your clarity, your edge, your tomorrow's energy for tonight's escape.

One day—October 1, 2023, to be exact—you're going to pour a very expensive bottle of whisky down the kitchen sink. Your kids (yeah, you have kids, and they're incredible) are going to be the reason. You're going to realize that being their hero matters more than being numb.

Do me a favor, okay? Find a different way to handle the pressure now. The standards you're about to learn? They work a lot better with a clear head.

THE BUSINESS WORLD'S WAITING

This is going to sound crazy, but hockey's just your apprenticeship. The real game comes after. All those contract negotiations you're going to hate? You're learning business. All those times you'll get traded? You're learning adaptation. All that leadership stuff you'll figure out on the ice and in the locker room? It translates perfectly to boardrooms.

You're going to own businesses. Not just invest— actually run them. That travel company with Lauren (your wife—and wait until you meet her, she's way out of your league but somehow you convinced her to say yes) is going to thrive because you'll apply the same standards to business that you learned in hockey.

You'll become a speaker. Yeah, you—the guy who gives two-word answers to media questions. Turns out, when you finally have something worth saying, people listen.

THE TRUTH ABOUT WHERE THIS LEADS

Here's what I really want you to know: Every single thing that's happening to you right now is exactly what needs to happen. That sports psychologist who's about to ask you about your standards? Listen to him. Those four words are going to change everything.

You're going to transform from a booed kid into a Hall of Famer. You're going to win a Stanley Cup. You're going to be named one of the one hundred greatest players in NHL history. You're going to impact thousands of lives through your speaking and writing.

But more importantly, you're going to become someone who owns his failures, learns from adversity, and helps others do the same. You're going to be a husband and father who shows up every day. You're going to be the mentor to others that Beast will be for you when you meet him.

So tonight, when you're lying there replaying every mistake, remember this: Champions aren't made by avoiding failure. They're made by surviving it, learning from it, and using it as fuel.

Champions aren't made by avoiding failure. They're made by surviving it, learning from it, and using it as fuel.

Those boos? They're not the end of your story. They're the beginning of everything that matters.

Trust the process, even when it hurts like hell.

Especially when it hurts like hell.

—Chris

P.S. In 1997, this company called Apple is going to be near bankruptcy. Everyone will say they're done. Buy the stock anyway. Buy a lot of it. You'll thank me in 2007 when something called an iPhone comes out. Also, that Gretzky rookie card you're thinking about selling? Don't.

ACKNOWLEDGMENTS

My deepest appreciation goes to the following incredibly special people whose influence over the years has made a huge positive difference in my life and career.

Bob & Kathy Crispin and your entire family. When I first arrived in Hartford as a young player, uncertain and trying to find my footing, you opened your home and your hearts to me. This book would not be complete without acknowledging the enormous impact you've had on my journey. Thank you for being such an incredible part of my life story.

Roger & Debbie White and family. When I arrived in Peterborough as a teenager chasing a dream, you welcomed me into your home and into your family. I will always be grateful for the love and kindness you showed me, and I'm proud to call you lifelong friends and family. You played a pivotal role in my journey, and this book would not be complete without thanking you for the incredible impact you had on my life.

Brad McCrimmon (Beast). Your impact on my life and career is something I will carry with me forever. More than a teammate, you were a true friend. I am forever grateful for your belief in me and for the example you set. This book would not be complete without honoring the profound role you played in my journey. I think about the phrase WWBD (what would Beast do?) often!

The A-Team: Mit, Hummer, Rock, Herbie, Murph, Ollie. Thank you for being the truest friends anyone could ask for. From the very beginning, you've been there through the highs and the lows, the wins and the setbacks, the good times and the tough ones.

You've been a constant source of laughter, perspective, and loyalty, and I wouldn't have wanted to take this journey without you by my side.

All my teammates over the years. The game gave me incredible opportunities, but what made the journey truly special were the people I shared the ice with. I'm deeply grateful for the friendships, the memories, and the lessons we shared. No one gets to the top alone, and I wouldn't trade the experiences we had for anything.

All the athletic trainers, equipment managers, and staff who worked behind the scenes throughout the years.

I owe you more than I could ever put into words. You were the glue that held everything together, and without you, none of us would have been able to compete the way we did. Thank you for your dedication, your professionalism, your friendship, and for everything you did to keep me in the game.

All my coaches. From my earliest days in hockey to the highest levels of the game, each of you played a role in shaping me, pushing me, and demanding more when I thought I had nothing left to give. I carry the lessons you taught me to this day, and I will always be grateful for the time, energy, and belief you poured into me.

All the GMs and owners I had the privilege of playing for. I will always be grateful for the confidence you showed in me and for allowing me to represent your organizations. Those years on the ice were some of the greatest of my life, and your support made them possible.

The City of Hartford and all Whalers fans. As a young player trying to find my way, your passion, support, and belief meant everything. Hartford was where it all started, and I'll always be grateful to the city and its people for giving me my first home in the National Hockey League.

The City of St. Louis and all the Blues fans everywhere. Thank you for embracing me and my family as one of your own. I am forever grateful to this city and its incredible fans for making those years so special, and for continuing to support me long after my playing days ended.

The City of Edmonton and the rabid Oilers fans. My time with the Oilers may have been short, but it was unforgettable. Thank you for embracing me and for allowing me to share in something so special. It was an honor to be part of Oil Country, and I'll always be grateful for the memories we created together.

The City of Anaheim, Orange County, and Ducks fans. Our 2007 Stanley Cup championship run will forever be one of my proudest [hockey] moments. This city and this team left an indelible mark on my life. I will always be grateful to the Ducks and to the people of Orange County for being such a meaningful part of my story.

The City of Philadelphia and Flyers Nation everywhere. From the moment I arrived, you inspired me to be better, demanded everything I had, and in return gave me your respect and unwavering support. Thank you for embracing me, challenging me, and making me feel part of your family.

And last but certainly not least, **The Fans.** Whether you loved me or hated me, you were always vocal, and I wouldn't have wanted it any other way. The energy, the emotion, and the love you bring to the rink are what make this sport great, and I am forever grateful to have been part of it. Thank you for your love of the game, and for making this journey one I will never forget.